THE BEST WORST CHRISTMAS EVER

THOMAS J. THORSON

The Best Worst Christmas Ever
Copyright © 2025 Thomas J. Thorson
ISBN: 978-1-7358366-9-0

Cover and internal illustrations © 2025 Stephanie Rocha
Cover and internal design © 2025 Stephanie Rocha / cafeychurros.com
The artwork was drawn by hand and colored digitally.

All rights reserved.
Printed in the United States of America.
No part of this book may be reproduced
in any manner whatsoever without permission.

bestworstchristmas.com

THE BEST WORST CHRISTMAS EVER

THOMAS J. THORSON

Contents

One: Snowbound 1
Two: A Most Unusual Dinner 9
Three: Lily Begins: Of Course There's a Fairy 21
Four: Candace Takes Over and the Quest Begins 25
Five Parker's Story: Gryla Lane 33

Santa's Missing Box

One: The Worst Christmas Ever 44
Two: The Assignment 51
Three: Sprig 59
Four: A Surprise Meeting 64
Five: The Town of No Name 69
Six: The Spice Shop and Another Surprise 75
Seven: The Library 85
Eight: Musical Clue 91
Nine: Reading the Tree 98
Ten: Following the Tinsel Trail 103
Eleven: The Mage 113
Twelve: Snowmen Show the Way 119
Thirteen: Themselves 127
Fourteen: Trolls and Bridges 133
Fifteen: The Christmas Market 141
Sixteen: The North Pole 147

Six: Christmas 153
Acknowledgments **157**

One

Snowbound

The scene looked like it had been lifted from the front of a holiday greeting card. A cozy cottage sat nestled at the edge of a wood of evergreen trees, a thin trail of smoke rising from its chimney before getting scattered by the frigid, gusty wind. The dark green door and matching shutters contrasted sharply with the tall mounds of snow drifted up against the sides of the home and piled high as far as the eye could see. Colored lights shone dimly through the frosty windowpanes and the outline of a pinecone wreath on the door was barely visible through the fierce flurry of heavy flakes. A solitary winter hare hurried for the safety and warmth of its burrow, its tracks quickly covered in a layer of snow. It was Christmas Eve, a night when both the creatures of the forest and the occupants of the cottage should have been nestled safely in the warmth of their homes, grateful for the tranquility that their shelter provided from the raging storm outside.

Inside this cottage, however, a glum silence reigned, only broken by the tapping of keys and an occasional moan, first from one spot, then from another, then from three different places at once. The joyful glimmer of the tree and radiance of the fire reflecting off the spirited holiday décor did nothing to raise the moods of the three children scattered around the living and dining rooms. Each of them stared unhappily at the screen of a laptop computer or phone, barely registering what was passing before their eyes. Their minds were focused elsewhere.

"It's not fair!" Parker said for the fourteenth time, to no one in particular. He lay restlessly across the couch, his feet dangling over its arm, a laptop balanced on his chest. At seventeen, he was tall for his age, but gangly and awkward, his overly thin frame still waiting to fill out and hesitant to bend to his wishes. As a result, he was always bumping into tables and stumbling over imaginary lines, to his sisters' amusement. He quickly forgave Lily for her giggles at his expense since she was only six but resented both Candace's smirks and her natural talent for athletics.

"I could have been on the beach right now," Candace whined as she scrolled social media on her phone for posts from girls her age luxuriating on tropical sands. "My friends would have been so jealous." Unlike Parker, who preferred keeping his own company or that of his one good friend, Candace was one of the most popular girls in her freshman class, if not the entire school. She excelled at three sports, got straight A's in everything but English, and was transitioning from a cute little girl into a pretty young woman. To Parker's annoyance, she also wasn't shy about trumpeting her achievements whenever he was within hearing distance.

"I'm bored," Lily said as she closed her tablet. "Daddy, can you call the airport again?"

John Natale gazed at the desperation in his daughter's eyes, knowing that nothing he could say would give her even a glimmer of the hope she sought. Best to just tell the truth, he thought to himself. "When I called a couple of hours ago," he said gently, "they told me that the airport was completely snowed in and wouldn't reopen until tomorrow at the earliest and probably not even then. Since that time, we've received at least a couple more inches and the storm has gotten even worse. I'm afraid Bermuda will have to wait for another time."

Although he was addressing Lily, his response drew sighs and mutterings from all directions. His earlier efforts to lighten the mood and distract his children by offering to play family games or to indulge in some sort of group activity fell flat. It wasn't surprising. Even at the best of times, it was rare for all three to get along with each other. Tension was always brewing between the two oldest, and arguing loudly or trying to find new ways to hurt their sibling had been the norm for at least a year or two. They usually excluded Lily from their feuds, but, like any child her age, she could sometimes be bratty and at those times all three would be at war with one another. For now, he'd let the kids work through their frustrations about missing out on their vacation before he again tried to bring everyone together. In the meantime, he returned to his book and left them to the distractions of the internet or to text their friends to complain about how awful their lives were.

The storm continued unabated as minutes turned into hours and the somber mood of the household held its grip. The children remained immersed in their own worlds except for the occasional griping that Parker was making irritating noises, or Lily took the last can of cola, or Candace had an evil smile on her face, which surely meant that she was saying awful things about Parker to her friends. Dad was about to lecture everyone about maintaining the Christmas spirit when it happened.

The first sign of trouble came in the late afternoon with a sudden cry of despair from Candace followed by her furious banging on the keys of her cell phone. As dad looked up from his book to identify the problem, he watched as Parker, who had seemed glued to his position on the couch for hours, rose and moved to the nearest window, where he held his laptop up against the glass. Lily walked over to where Dad was sitting and held out her tablet.

"Daddy, can you fix this?" she asked. Dad took the tablet in hand and, once he saw the message on the screen along with interpreting the actions of his other two children, quickly discovered the cause of the angst. The Wi-Fi was down. Moving swiftly before chaos took hold, he dashed to his office to see what he could do, but the news there was grim. It wasn't just the Wi-Fi. The entire internet was down.

Every eye was on him as he emerged from the office. His expression must have revealed what he was about to say given the looks of horror on the faces of his children. He said it anyway. "I'm afraid we have no internet. My guess is that it won't be back up until the storm ends and workers can do whatever they need to do to fix it.

"I know you've been looking forward to our trip for months," he said, "but there's nothing we can do about the weather and we need to make the best of our misfortune. I'm going to propose that we play games together, only this time it's not a suggestion." Parker and Candace didn't give any sign that they'd heard him. "C'mon, we used to do this every Friday night and it was a lot of fun."

"I don't remember that," Lily said. "Was I alive then?"

"Yes," Dad told her, "but you were really young and didn't understand the rules. Candace and Parker, do you remember? When she was a toddler we'd give Lily game pieces and cards from a different game than the one we were playing so that she'd feel included and when we finished we'd tell her that she'd won."

Despite themselves, small smiles of recognition crept over the faces of the two older children. Lily, however, was appalled. He eyes grew wide. "Wait, Daddy. You mean—"

"Parker, why don't you go into the basement and bring up a few games," Dad said quickly, cutting Lily off. "Something we can all play," he added as he looked at Lily. Moments later, the dining room table had been cleared and a pile of dusty games sat in front of them.

"You only brought up games that you used to win," Candace said angrily to Parker.

"You only like those girly games or ones that you play with your friends so that you get an advantage," Parker retorted.

"Daddy, I don't want to play any of these. They look too hard," Lily whined.

After ten minutes of bickering and accusations flying back and forth between the older children and Lily loudly complaining that they were ignoring what she wanted because she was little, Dad brokered a peace by picking a game that none of them chose and offering to be on a team with Lily. Candace and Parker were put in charge of setting up the game board and dealing out the cards. Dad moved close to Lily and began reading the instructions. Five minutes later, after more disagreement as to who would go first, Lily picked up the dice and rolled them onto the board.

That's when the lights went out.

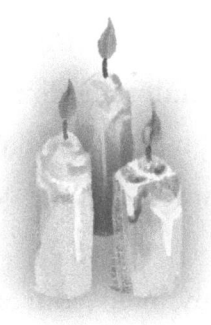

Two

A Most Unusual Dinner

For a moment all was quiet in the darkness. Then, as if on cue, three voices broke the silence at the same time. Lily squeaked, Candace squawked, and Parker muttered something he shouldn't have. Dad sat back, pulled Lily onto his lap, and ran his fingers through his hair before taking charge.

"Parker, please round up as many candles as you can find. There should be quite a few in the kitchen junk drawer, and don't forget the holiday candles we use for decoration that are scattered all around the house. When you're done, bring them into the living room. Candace, please grab the fuzzy gray blanket out of the chest in my bedroom, then bring the comforters, blankets, and pillows from all our beds. Lily and I will be putting a few more logs on the fire to get it blazing for warmth and some additional light."

In a flash, small beams of light from three cell phones blazed trails in three different directions. As the new logs caught fire, sending high bursts of flames skyward, a walking tower of bedcovers stumbled in the general direction of Dad and Lily.

Dad chuckled. "Lily, help your sister please." Soon the three of them spread the fuzzy blanket over the floor as a base then folded the comforters, stacking them in sets of two close to the fire with multiple pillows piled behind them to act as back rests, leaving the blankets to wrap around their shoulders. Parker joined them as they were finishing up, carrying a heavy shopping bag.

"There must have been a sale on wax and you stocked up," he said as he set the bag of candles down with a loud thud. "Where do you want them?"

"Set them aside until we need them," Dad replied. "For now, let's get cozy and warm and figure out what we're going to do next."

Each of the children settled onto the makeshift couches and wrapped themselves up in their own favorite blanket before looking around at their siblings, waiting for someone else to say something. Eventually all three of them turned their attention toward Dad.

"We could play a word game, or you could talk about what's been going on with you at school," he suggested. The silence that filled the room in response to his suggestion told him all he needed to know. He'd have to think of something else.

"Actually, I'm a little hungry," Parker said.

"I'm starving!" Lily added.

"I guess I could eat," Candace admitted. "What are we having for dinner?"

"I've been wondering about that myself," Dad said. "I was going to surprise you with a special Christmas meal using food I was saving for New Years, but it requires an oven. Or at least a burner or two in a pinch. But our stove is electric. We have no way to cook it."

"So, we're going to starve on Christmas Eve?" Parker said glumly. "That's nice."

"Well, I do have one idea," Dad said with a smile. "But I don't know if you'd go for it. The main ingredient is imagination and I'm not sure you're up for the challenge."

"I know what you're doing," Candace said, eyeing her father suspiciously. "You're trying to bait us. To motivate us to do whatever you're proposing in order to prove that we could do it." She paused to think. "And it's working, but only because all this talk about food and the possibility of not eating at all is making me ravenous. What do you have in mind?"

"Let's call it our 'Desperation Dinner.' We don't know how long the power will be out, and I'd hate to have all our food spoil. For once we're not going to worry about a balanced meal, or what's good for us, or calories. Each one of you will be assigned a course and anything goes. Give priority to food that we might lose due to the power outage, but beyond that there are no rules. Be creative. How does that sound?"

They tried not to show their excitement, but each of the children's minds was already racing with the possibilities.

"I guess we could give that a try," Parker said, trying to keep his voice level so as not to give Dad the satisfaction of having come up with a good idea on the fly. "Just remember that you said no rules."

"I remember," Dad agreed. "Parker, you have the appetizer, Candace you have the main course, and Lily you have dessert. I'll set up some candles around the house and will bring out the plates and glasses. After that you're on your own. Ready?"

Dad soon found himself alone by the fire sitting cross-legged on a comforter while listening to a constant flow of noise from the kitchen ranging from raised voices to conspiratorial whispers and the sounds of pots and utensils dropping on the counter. At least they weren't fighting, he thought. They were being forced to work together to defeat a common enemy, in this case the effects of Mother Nature. He was curious as to what their imaginations would conjure up and braced himself for pickles on toast or crushed crackers topped with hot fudge and applesauce.

It wasn't long before the three children marched single file back into the living room. Lily led the way carrying a bowl in each hand followed by Candace, who also toted two bowls. Parker trailed behind with a large serving platter held high. They stopped opposite their father but made no effort to place the food on the blanket. From his position on the floor, Dad was unable to see what delights the bowls and plate held. He sniffed the air but couldn't detect any recognizable aroma.

Parker edged forward. "As you know, sir," he announced formally, "the first course was up to me. Tonight we present the house special. Soup." As he finished, Lily and Candace lowered themselves to the ground and positioned the bowls at each place setting. Parker immediately followed up by putting the platter in the center of the blanket.

Dad looked at the contents of his bowl. "This is ice cream," he said.

"Think of it as the early stages of soup," Parker replied. "Kind of a chocolate chip and strawberry pre-soup." As if to prove his point, the warmth of the fire began to liquify the edges of the scoops of ice cream, threatening to melt the bowls' contents completely if left uneaten for any length of time. "And we've provided an assortment of crackers to add if you wish."

Dad looked up from his bowl and examined the "cracker" plate filled with candy cane pieces, crumbles of cookies, graham crackers, and some peanuts. Well, he did give them full control to come up with something and the idea of "pre-soup" was growing on him. He reached out and grabbed a handful of cookie crumbs, stirring them into the now half-melted contents of his bowl and quickly dipped his spoon into the mix.

That was the signal for the children to dig in as well. Conversation gave way to giggling and laughter mixed with slurping sounds. Parker eventually ditched his spoon and lifted his bowl to his lips, leaving a ring of pink and brown liquid around his mouth. He resembled a circus clown, Candace remarked. Lily laughed so hard she snorted ice cream out her nose.

"I give Round 1 five stars!" Dad exclaimed, drawing a grin from the chef. "What's next?"

In response, the trio gathered up the dishes and the remnants of the "crackers" and retreated to the kitchen. This time, the wait was longer. As before, the kids entered in a straight line one after the other. Lily walked with her arms behind her back, Parker carried the same platter as the last time, again too high to see what it held, and Candace's hands held several bottles and jars. It was too dark to see what they contained.

She stepped around her siblings and placed one container in front of each person's place on the floor. Dad could now make out what they were but identifying them did nothing to reveal what role they would play in the meal. Ketchup, a jar of mustard, hot sauce, and pesto. Not exactly anything that should be eaten on their own. Candace cleared her throat.

"For tonight's main course, we present customized grilled cheese sandwiches," she announced. "In other words, you choose your own ingredients, assemble your sandwich, then my grill master—that's you, Dad—will roast them over an open fire."

As she finished speaking, Parker once more lowered the platter to the blanket. One side was crammed with cheese: deli slices of cheddar and Swiss as well as crudely sliced pieces of Havarti and mozzarella. In the center of the plate were leftover pieces of pepperoni from a pizza they'd made the week before, sandwich ham, and bacon from yesterday's breakfast. The far side of the platter held black olive halves, cornichon pickles, pepperoncini, and a jar of raspberry jam. A stick of butter, softening rapidly near the fire, rounded out the selection.

"Wow," Dad said, flabbergasted. "I've never—"

Before he could finish, three pairs of hands flew to the bread as the children began assembling their dinners. Dad watched amused and slightly nauseated as he saw combinations of meats with jam, layers of pickles, multiple sauces, and, in Lily's case, a few simple slices of cheese with a dot of ketchup in the center. Buttering the bread after the sandwiches were already made was a messy affair, but eventually all four creations were ready to be placed into the grill basket conveniently stored next to the fireplace.

"This is your course, Candace, so I'm passing the honors over to you," Dad said as he passed the handle of the basket to her. "Although I do suggest that you hold them over the embers near the front here instead of plunging them into the flames. Parker, your job is to control the embers to avoid flareups."

By the time Candace pulled the sandwiches out of the fireplace, there were a few burnt spots and cascades of gooey cheese had melted out of Parker's overly filled sandwich, but the group agreed that they had never had grilled cheese that tasted quite as good or that required quite as many napkins.

As she drank the remnants of her second can of ginger ale, Candace gave a small burp. "Do we have to have dessert?" she moaned. "I'm full." Parker belched in assent.

"You're only saying that because it's my turn!" Lily objected. She stood up and began marching off in the direction of the kitchen before turning back, putting her hands firmly on her hips. "And you have to come and help me."

After their pleading eyes drew no relief from Dad, the two teenagers reluctantly got to their feet, gathered up the dinner dishes, and followed Lily. Parker returned seconds later. "Dad, where are those long campfire sticks we used for roasting hot dogs last summer?"

"I think they're hanging off a hook at the back of the shelf near the bamboo steamer," he replied. "Please tell me we're not having hot dogs for dessert."

Parker smiled and left without responding. It was only minutes later that the whole crew returned. The bag of marshmallows Lily carried proudly gave away the surprise, but Dad didn't let on that he knew.

"S'mores!" Lily announced as she dropped the marshmallows onto the blanket.

"Except we used up all of the graham crackers for the soup," Candace said. "So we're using flour tortillas."

Parker threaded two marshmallows each onto four metal sticks while Dad placed the tortillas into the grill basket, still messy from the last course. "We might get a little bit of cheese as a bonus," he said. "I'll heat these up if one of you can do my marshmallows."

A short minute later Dad pulled the warm tortillas off the fire and placed a chocolate bar onto each one. Lily was the first to pull her fiery, blackened marshmallows out of the fire. Parker followed shortly afterward, all four marshmallows on his sticks immersed in flame. Dad quickly slid all three pairs onto the tortillas and handed them to his children to wrap up. Candace insisted on trying to roast her marshmallows slowly until they were perfectly browned on all sides, but upon hearing the sounds of ecstasy as her brother and sister bit into their s'mores, allowed them to be consumed by the fire and soon joined them in expressing her appreciation for the treat.

A satisfied silence followed dinner, eventually broken by Dad. "It's Christmas Eve, so the dishes can wait," he said. "Why don't you bring the dessert dishes out to the kitchen, I'll put another log on the fire, and we'll decide what to do next."

When the group was once more gathered around the fire,

all three children looked at their Dad, waiting for him to take the initiative. He, in turn, waited for the children to offer suggestions. When the silence finally became too awkward, Dad spoke.

"So no ideas? We're a bit limited without power or Wi-Fi, and even if we lit up every candle we have, there's not enough light to play any game that involves playing pieces or cards. That basically means talking is our only option. Unless you want to sing Christmas carols."

"Please, Dad, don't ask us again to talk about school or anything related to school," Candace said. "As you said, it's Christmas Eve, and that should be the farthest thing from our minds. And I've heard Parker sing. No thanks. We need to do something happier."

"And maybe Christmas related," Parker added.

"Let's tell a story," Lily said with more enthusiasm than the rest of the group felt. "But it has to be one I know, like Rudolph or Frosty or something."

Her idea was met with groans from her sister and brother. Before they could verbally express their dislike of Lily's idea, causing more friction, Dad stepped in.

"It's not the worst idea," he said thoughtfully. "Although maybe we don't want to retell someone else's story, or one that we've heard over and over. We could create our own Christmas tale. When I was younger some friends and I wrote a story where one of us started it then passed it on to the next in line, who added to it, until everyone contributed.

A collaborative effort, like links in a chain. The fun part is trying to continue the story in a way that makes sense but adds your own touch to each part of it."

His words were met with dubious looks from all three, so he had to try to sell the plan. "It's not like we've come up with any other ideas," he continued. "We could at least give it a try, and if at any time it turns out to be just another one of Dad's dumb suggestions, we'll try something else."

"I guess we could at least start, until someone thinks of something better," Parker said. "Who goes first?"

"It should be Lily," Candace said, "since it'll be hard for her to pick up the plot in the middle of the story. Besides, storytelling was her idea so she should decide what kind of a story it's going to be."

Lily demonstrated what a great idea she thought this was by bouncing up and down on her share of the comforter. Before she could begin, Dad intervened.

"Lily, you can take a few minutes to think of how you want to start the story," he said. "There something I need to do first. While she's thinking, Candace and Parker I need you to pull eight empty soda cans out of recycling and bring them in here along with an oven rack, three sturdy candles, and four mugs. I'll be right behind you."

Candace and Parker were puzzled but knew better than to ask questions when Dad was in a mischievous mood, so they quickly assembled the requested items. Dad returned from the kitchen minutes later carrying a large saucepan and wooden spoon. Without saying a word, he made four stacks of two pop cans each in a rectangular pattern in a spot on the floor away from the fire then placed the oven rack on top. Checking first that the rack was sturdy and balanced, he placed the saucepan in the middle of it then lined up the candles on the floor beneath the pan.

"Hot chocolate," he said as he lit the candles. "My own special recipe. Without a stovetop, it's going to take time to heat and for the flavors to blend, but it gives us something to look forward to. We'll take turns stirring."

His task complete, Dad returned to his spot near the fire. "Have you thought of how to start the story, Lily? Good. Then let's begin."

Three

Lily Begins: Of Course There's a Fairy

"Now remember," Dad told Lily, "it's just the beginning of the story. Don't tell the whole thing, you have to leave us somewhere to go. In some ways it's the most important part because you get to decide what kind of story it's going to be before you turn it over to the rest of us to continue on."

Lily beamed. "Once upon a time..." she began.

"Oh boy," Parker groaned.

"Quiet, Parker," Candace scolded. "That's how a lot of the best stories start off."

"Once upon a time," Lily said again, "there was a girl named Lily and she was six years old. She liked unicorns and polar bears and baking cookies and she was very smart.

Everybody liked her because she was so nice and polite. She was good at art and remembering things and following directions."

"Those are her superpowers?" Parker asked in disbelief. He opened his mouth to say something else but halted when he saw Dad shake his head slightly. Lily ignored her brother and stared into the fire, deciding what came next.

"Don't forget this is a Christmas story," Dad prompted.

"Oh yeah," Lily said. "It was five and a half days before Christmas and she was playing with dolls in her room when a fairy floated through her window. Lily wasn't scared because she was a friendly fairy. She was wearing a pink and purple and yellow dress with sparkles and her wings were sparkly too. 'Lily,' she said, because she knew my—she knew the girl's name, 'Santa Claus needs your help and said you're the only girl in the whole world who will know what to do. He sent me to get you. You need to come to the North Pole with me.'"

"I guess this isn't just a fairy tale, it's a tale about fairies," Candace said.

"Hush," Dad told her.

Lily took a big breath before continuing. "So Lily took the fairy's hand and they flew together to the North Pole. Lily was cold but the fairy used magic to make a warm coat made out of reindeer fur for her."

"Reindeer don't have fur," Parker grumbled.

"Quiet, Parker," Candace said. "Be nice. And yes they

do, even on their antlers. Go on, Lily."

"When they landed there were elves everywhere and the girl could smell gingerbread. The fairy told Lily to follow her and they walked past a building where more elves were making toys and then a bakery with a window full of cookies until they entered a house with a really big red and green door. The fairy took her into a room with a fireplace that took up a whole wall and in one corner was a Christmas tree that went all the way up to the ceiling. It was full of pretty ornaments and candy canes and there were presents all around it."

Lily stopped talking long enough for Dad to wonder if she had finished. "Before you let someone else continue," he said gently, "are you going to tell us why Santa needed to talk with Lily?"

"Ok," Lily said, wrinkling her nose as she thought hard. "There was a chair just Lily's size by the fire so she sat in it to get warm. Mrs. Claus came in and said 'You must be Lily' and gave her a plate of cookies and a hot drink that tasted like apples and cinnamon. Seven minutes later Santa came in. He was big and fat but had a nice smile.

"'Lily,' Santa said, 'I have a problem. For a lot of years I kept a box in my workshop that had something very, very, very important in it but this morning it was gone.'"

"What was gone?" Candace asked. "The box or what was inside?"

"And can you tell us what was in the box?" Parker added.

"It was a piece of paper with something written on it but it was secret so Santa couldn't tell her," Lily responded, getting irritated with her siblings. "And the whole box was gone. Stop asking questions. I'm not done telling my part yet.

"'Christmas Eve is coming soon and I want that box back before I fly around the world,' Santa told Lily. 'I looked at my list of all the nice kids and saw your name and I knew that you were the right girl for the job. Will you help me?' And Lily said 'Of course I will, Santa' and she jumped out of her chair. 'Take me to your workshop,' I said."

"You mean 'Lily said,'" Parker interjected.

"That's what I meant," Lily answered indignantly. "So she went to the workshop that was full of wood and dust and the fairy came with her to help and they started looking for clues."

Lily paused. "That's all," she decided.

"It's a nice start," Dad said as he rose to stir the hot chocolate. "I love a good mystery and I can't wait to hear what comes next. Who's going to take up the story from here?"

Parker and Candace looked at each other. "I will," Candace said. "We'll go in ascending order by age."

Parker added another log to the fire, all four pulled their blankets tight, and Candace cleared her throat. "I'm going to back up just a little," she said.

Four

Candace Takes Over and the Quest Begins

"The elves' workshop was the size of three soccer fields," she began. "Lily stared through a window at a thousand elves working at long tables covered in sawdust and paint. The supervising elves wore gold smocks while the rest of them were dressed in green and red tunics. The entire room seemed to be in motion and the noise they made was painful to hear even through the heavy glass. Lily put her hands over her ears, bracing herself before going inside.

"'Don't worry,' Santa told her. 'That's not where we're going.' As he spoke Santa pulled a long silver key from his pocket and continued walking down the snowy lane until the sound of the elves was just a murmur. He stopped before a wooden door that was as wide as it was tall and fit the key into the lock in the doorknob. With a squeak and a creak, the door slowly opened inward and Santa led Lily and the fairy inside.

"Lily gasped as she looked around the room. While smaller than the elves' workshop, it was still as big as a large classroom but seemed smaller because everywhere she looked there was something wonderful to look at. A long, wide table running from the outside door to the far side of the room was covered by tools, odd equipment whose purpose she couldn't imagine, half-finished toys, scraps of paper with drawings and doodles, and a large, heavy book labeled 'Naughty and Nice.' Along every wall were shelves that rose so high Lily couldn't see their tops. They too were jammed full of toys and trinkets. A giant Christmas tree stood in one corner, shiny red and green ornaments reflecting the white lights draped around it. Lily could barely make out her fairy friend sitting on a branch at the very top of the tree.

"Santa led Lily halfway down the length of the table, where a space had been cut out in the middle to fit a heavy swivel chair. Santa eased himself into the chair and directed Lily to pull up a nearby stool.

"'This is where I come when I want to be alone,' Santa explained. 'The quiet lets me ease my mind by fiddling with ideas for new toys or just for the joy of working with wood. No one outside of Mrs. Claus and myself even know that this workshop exists, or at least we thought so. That's why it made such a perfect place to keep something as valuable as the missing box I need you to find. It blended in with all the rest of the objects on the shelves. You'd have to know what to look for to locate it. You can see the empty space over on that shelf, between the antique top and the airplane with the painted wings.'

"'What did the box look like?' the fairy asked Santa."

"No, not the fairy," Lily insisted, interrupting her sister. "Lily asked that."

"Fine," Candace sighed. "But let me tell the story my way from now on. 'What did the box look like?' Lily asked because she was smarter than the fairy.

"'It was nothing remarkable,' Santa answered. 'It was small, not much bigger than the length of your hand, and only as tall as your thumb. It was made of cherry, oak, and mahogany wood, so it was multi-colored, and it was as smooth as ice on a frigid winter's day. That's all I can tell you, except that it was here yesterday and today it isn't. Now I need to leave you because, as I'm sure you understand, I'm very busy this time of year.'

"After Santa left, the fairy flew over to examine the spot where the box had been. Lily had to drag a ladder over because even though she was smarter than the fairy she was also short and she couldn't fly."

"Hey," Lily whined.

"Careful, Candace," Dad warned. "No snarky comments please. Other than that you're doing well. Please go on."

"The first thing that Lily and the fairy noticed was that

there were smudges left in the sawdust that lined every shelf of the workshop," Candace continued. "So Lily took pictures of them with her phone. 'It must have been an elf because who else could it be?' Lily guessed out loud. 'If you took something really valuable and wanted to hide it, where would you put it?'

"The fairy gave the question some thought. 'The elves don't really have any personal space, and they're almost never any place where twenty or thirty other elves aren't nearby. It would be difficult, maybe even impossible, to hide something in the first place and even if you could, someone would stumble onto it. No, whoever took it must have taken it somewhere outside the compound.'

"'But where else is there?' Lily asked because even though she was smart she was also ignorant of the geography of the North Pole. Quiet, Lily, this is my turn. 'The most logical place would be North Pole Village,' the fairy answered. 'It's about six minutes away by sled and the closest town to here by hundreds of miles.'"

"Just a suggestion," Dad intervened. "Do you think the fairy could have a name?"

"Ooh! Ooh! I know! I know!" Lily said excitedly. "Belinda! No, Swizzle!"

"Sorry, sis," Candace answered. "My story, my choice. Her name is Fayetta, or Fae for short. Now let me go on please.

"Lily and the fairy bundled back up in their coats and

Fayetta suggested that they put scarves around their faces because the sled ride would be cold. They left the workshop and walked five hundred steps past the last building, which was the cafeteria, where they found dozens of sleds in all sizes and colors stored inside a shed. They chose a purple one with a silver streak. Lily dragged it to the top of the slope, tucked Fae inside the front of her coat, and they pushed off and took off down the hill.

"The blades of the sled threw up snow in their faces as they descended, blinding Lily while she tried to steer. She felt rather than saw the sled glide onto even ground but they continued to travel fast. Lily was worried they would hit someone so she dug her heels in on either side of the sled, which caused it to stop suddenly and throw the riders high up into the air. Fortunately they landed in a soft snowbank. They didn't know what happened to the sled. They never saw it again.

"'Are you okay?' asked a voice. Lily wiped snow off her eyes and Fae emerged from inside her coat and they saw a beautiful young woman with clear blue eyes staring at them. 'I watched you fly over me and thought you must be magical because people can't fly and you don't have wings anyway.'

"'Hmmph,' Fae said, insulted. That's when the girl saw the fairy and she was astonished because fairies were never seen in this town. 'My name's Candace,' the young woman said."

"Of course it is," Parker mumbled.

"'You must be frozen,' Candace said to Lily and Fae. 'I know a little place nearby with a giant fireplace and good soup where you can warm up inside and out. Follow me.'

"Inside the café Lily and Fae were happy to be rescued by someone as kindhearted as Candace and they instinctively knew that they could trust her. So while they were eating soup by the fire they told her about their mission to find Santa's missing box.

"'Art is my main interest but I'm also pretty good at solving puzzles,' Candace said. 'Would you like me to help?'

"Lily and Fae were of course happy to have another person join them on their mission and immediately asked her if she knew where they could start looking for the box.

"Candace thought for a minute. 'Well, I do have one idea,' she said. 'There's a nearby shop I like to go to because it sells a little bit of everything and even if I go there two days in a row nothing on their shelves looks familiar. It's as if they empty out and put all new stuff in there overnight. A lot of it is very unusual. Maybe the owner will know something about the box. Maybe he even has it on one of his shelves.'

"Lily and Fae hated to leave the warmth of the fireplace and go back out into the cold, but it was a short walk to the shop and soon they were inside again. And what a marvelous place it was! It reminded Lily of Santa's personal workshop because there wasn't an empty space anywhere except that everything here was finished and was only waiting for a home.

"The man behind the counter was odd looking, with ears

as big as saucers and eyes that looked like giant cookies with a chocolate chip in the center. Candace said she would ask him about the box and began to speak. Lily and Fae looked at each other in confusion. They didn't understand what either of them was saying. When she'd finished, Candace told them that the shop owner was a cross between an elf, a gnome, and a unicorn and that he spoke a language that most people didn't understand. Fortunately, she spoke it fluently.

"'He said that a strange creature hidden beneath a flowing green cloak much too long for it was in here earlier today trying to sell him something that he kept hidden in his pocket, but he wouldn't buy it because the creature wouldn't tell him what he was selling until he got paid,' Candace told the others. 'And he was asking way too much money, justifying the cost by saying that it had special powers. The owner shooed him away and noticed that he turned left after leaving the shop.'

"Upon hearing that, the trio left the shop and started walking in the direction the creature had gone. 'Look!' said Candace. 'See on the ground, there's a drag mark. It must have been made by the cloak rubbing up against the snow. If we follow it, we can see where it went.'

"Lily and Fae agreed that Candace was ingenious to figure that out. They followed the marks in the snow until they disappeared into a—" At this point, Candace stopped talking.

"Into a what?" Parker asked.

"I don't know," Candace replied. "This is where my part of the story ends."

Parker's face fell and he cast a desperate look at his father. "That's fair," Dad said. "Think of it as an opportunity. Let's take a five-minute break and you can use that time to think of where they go."

Candace stood to stretch and moved over to the hot chocolate to give it a stir, leaning down to take a sniff. "Dad, what's in this?" she asked. "It smells different. Not bad, just different. Kind of interesting, actually."

"You'll have to wait and see if your taste buds pick out the ingredients," Dad replied. "For now, though, it still has to simmer longer."

Soon—all too soon for Parker—the family reassumed their places on the floor. Three sets of eyes turned to Parker as he wondered what he was going to say.

Five

Parker's Story: Gryla Lane

"Candace, can you repeat the last sentence where you left off the story?" Parker asked his sister, stalling for time. She obliged.

"Let's see. Lily, Fae, and Candace had just left the oddity shop and they followed drag marks in the snow until they disappeared into a..."

"'Nother dimension!" Parker finished, inspired by his choice.

"What?" Candace objected. "Dad!"

Dad smiled. "You did leave it open, Candace. I'm interested to see how this ties into the story."

"Me too," Lily added.

"The three girls turned a corner of the village and suddenly found themselves on a street that at first seemed to be a continuation of where they'd just been, but they soon noticed weird differences," Parker continued. "The homes and shops were shaped like fish bowls, with windows where the doors normally are and doors in place of windows. Small steps leading up to and between the doors on the upper levels snaked across the fronts of the homes. Each building as far as the group could see was a different color, creating a visual rainbow.

"Strangest of all, though, was what happened when they walked. With each step, the ground beneath their feet created a musical note. They soon discovered that if they left their foot in place, the tone lingered for several seconds, but if they took a few short steps the notes were short and in quick succession. Sometimes the notes were high, other times low. If there was a clue to how their walk created different notes on the scale, they couldn't figure it out. What they did know was that as they moved forward as a group, the resulting chorus of sounds they created was a jumble of noise that bore no resemblance to music. To save their ears from further insult, they stopped moving altogether and huddled together in a group.

"'It takes a while to get the hang of it,' a voice called out. A pleasant melody consisting of a mix of strings and horns got gradually louder as a young man walked briskly in their direction. 'Which notes you play depends on the placement of your foot when it touches the ground,' he explained. To demonstrate, he contorted his feet into unnatural positions as he approached, creating a two-octave scale with every note in perfect position.

"'My name is Parker,' he said. 'I woke up one morning wedged between two houses a couple of blocks away. That was maybe a month ago, and I've been here ever since. I'm really good at music and seeing patterns, so it didn't take me long to catch on to how this works.'

"Candace watched him closely as he approached and couldn't help but notice how handsome he was."

"Oh, please," Candace interjected. "Don't make me gag. Just stick to the story."

Parker ignored her.

"'We're a bit lost,' Lily told the boy. 'We were following somebody—'

"'Or something,' Fae added.

"'—when we turned a corner and ended up where we are now. Did you see a person or creature in a long cloak carrying a small box in its hands?'

"Parker put his chin in his hand and thought for a moment. 'Now that you mention it, I did see something matching that description not more than five minutes ago. It was headed in the direction of the clockmaker's shop. Follow me and I'll take you there.'

"The beautiful medley of Christmas carols Parker's footsteps made as he strode away was drowned out by the awful noise the group created, drawing the attention of the townspeople as they passed. They were small, rotund elfishlooking things, resembling walking beachballs with bright green eyes. The men all had colorful beards falling almost to their knees, the women colorful hair that extended nearly to the ground. 'Those colors match the houses where they reside,' Parker explained.

"The shop they soon entered was stocked with clocks of every description, from grandfather clocks that dwarfed the group and extended nearly to the ceiling to cuckoo clocks with choruses of birds singing, to small table models, but it was much more than that. Wooden hand-carved delights crammed the tables and shelves. Jewelry boxes, figurines of animals and people, and tree ornaments in a myriad of shapes and styles. It was a wonderous, magical place just waiting to be explored.

"'No wonder that thing brought Santa's box here,' Candace said. 'It would fit right in.'

"'Did you say Santa's box?' a gruff voice belted from behind a counter. 'Is that what that was? If I'd known, I would have taken it off the old man. It didn't look like anything special and he wanted a small fortune for it, so I sent him on his way.'

"Parker turned in the direction of the voice, where an old man with wrinkles on his wrinkles and a beard the color of a robin's egg stood. 'Can you tell us what he looked like and where he might have gone next?' Parker asked.

"'He was one of those ispidlic creatures, you know, from the tribe that lives in the ice caves up in the mountains,' the shopkeeper said. 'Don't see them much on this side of town. He looked ancient, probably well over 150 years old, but moved lightly. Didn't make a sound when he moved either, kind of glided above the surface. Purple eyes and hair as black as the coal naughty children get in their stockings. As far as where he went from here, all I can do is guess, but it's a pretty good guess. If you can brave it, he probably went to Gryla Lane. That's where dark business gets done, the kinds of transactions no one else will touch. If I were you, I'd just go back to the North Pole and tell Santa the box disappeared without a trace.'

"Downhearted, the group of four left the clock shop to decide what to do next. 'We can't give up,' Lily said. 'We can't let Santa down.'

"'I've heard of Gryla Lane,' Parker told them. 'It's not somewhere to go unprepared. But I have an idea.' Without another word, Parker started off down a side street lit only by a single streetlight. As soon as the three girls entered the street to follow him, no more music came when they walked. The air seemed heavy and their breathing echoed off every building they passed. The buildings themselves had lost their color, all of them gray and dingy and blending together."

"I don't like this," Lily interrupted. "You don't have to make the story this scary."

"Don't worry, Lily," Parker said. "No one gets hurt. Let me continue.

"Just when they thought their surroundings couldn't

get any darker, Parker stopped in front of a small, crooked hutch with a single, dim light in the window. Its door creaked ominously as he opened it and entered, with the others right behind him. The interior was all shadows and the faint scent of incense was in the air. Only as their eyes began to adjust did they notice a small figure hunched over on a chair in the corner, leaning forward on a walking stick. 'What brings you to Madame Fiscus?' she croaked.

"'We're on a mission for Santa,' Parker explained. 'And need to follow a lead into Gryla Lane. I understand you sell charms that may protect us while we're there.'

"At first the old woman didn't say anything more. Then she rose slowly, nodding her head as she did so. She disappeared into the back before returning with a small pendant from which hung a glowing reddish gem.

"'This will ward off the evil of that place,' she said. 'But only as long as it continues to glow, and I can't predict how long that will be. You need to be out of there before it dims.'

"Parker settled up with the woman and soon the group was making its way, with some trepidation, further down the lane, which somehow continued to darken more with each step. Parker came to a sudden stop, causing the group to bump into him from behind. He stared through the gloom in every direction before nodding his head slightly. He pointed to a barely visible gap between two crooked houses and started walking toward it, the rest following closely.

"About ten steps in the narrow gap widened far enough

to allow the four adventurers to walk side by side. Shops with dirty windows and no signage lined the walkway on both sides and furtive figures darted in the shadows. The group shuffled forward slowly, glancing in all directions for a clue as to what they should do next. Suddenly their way was blocked by a figure completely hidden inside a black cloak. All that was visible of the creature within was a long, knobby finger that emerged from one sleeve. It pointed to the entrance of a small building with a door no more than three and a half feet tall before disappearing as mysteriously as it appeared. Each member of the group grabbed the hand of the person next to them, and slowly, hesitantly, they moved toward the door."

Parker paused as his father and siblings perched on the edge of the comforter, waiting to hear what happened next. The flames of the fire danced, casting eerie shadows into the room. Parker looked each of his listeners in the eye, then grinned. "That's where I stop," he finally said.

"Of course it is," Candace said, disappointed in the break. "Dad, I guess it's up to you to bring it home."

"How about a bit of a break first," Dad replied. "Let's stretch, use the bathroom, and give me a few minutes to think. Lily, your turn to stir the hot chocolate. And no tasting."

Dad looked out the window at the blizzard as the others moved about the home. Candace threw two more logs on the fire as they settled back onto the comfort of the blankets, turning to their father in expectation.

"I appreciate where the three of you brought the story so far," he said, "but how would you feel if I start from the beginning? I promise to incorporate some of what you've created. It would make it easier to make it a bit more seamless."

None of the children objected and they drew their blankets closer around their shoulders. Dad took a deep breath, stared for a few moments into the fire, and began from the beginning.

Santa and the Missing Box

One

The Worst Christmas Ever

Candace threw herself onto her bed and buried her head in her pillow, screaming into its soft folds. At fourteen, she could still appreciate the traditions of the holiday season such as trimming the tree, teasing her sister about what might be inside the colorful packages carefully wrapped in secret, and drinking hot chocolate by the fire while listening to "Frosty the Snowman" for the hundredth time. But something was missing. She was having trouble capturing the magical feeling that Christmas instilled in her only a few years before.

Part of the problem may have been that with each passing year she was given more responsibility to bring Christmas into the family home. Carry boxes of wreaths and ornaments down from the attic, untangle the tree lights, inventory the cookie decorating supplies to make sure they wouldn't be short of red food coloring or sprinkles again this year, sweep up pine needles. The list went on and on. She was sure that her older brother Parker wasn't given half as much to do as she was and her resentment ran deep. And Lily? She didn't seem to have any jobs at all except to be as annoying as she wanted to be in the name of the Christmas spirit.

It didn't help that Candace's friends all seemed to conspire with each other to convince their families to plan exotic destination vacations over the holidays. Angela was skiing in Colorado, Monica was on a beach in Mexico, and two other girls were having the times of their lives at Disney World. And here she was, stuck at home with snow piled a thousand feet high outside being forced to play nice with her siblings. Her life was so dull. Nothing exciting or even out of the ordinary ever happened to her. This would be the worst Christmas ever.

She flopped over onto her back and stared at the ceiling, her eyes coming to rest on the small dark patch discolored by a minor roof leak last summer. She hated its ugliness. Her dad had promised at least a dozen times to fix it, but there it was in all its hideous glory staring down at her. The way things were shaking out, he'd probably ask her to add it to her already long list of tasks.

She could hear Lily singing along with some dumb carol downstairs and the incessant noise of Parker's latest video game from his room next to hers. Her dad must be in the kitchen, as the aromas of bread and some sort of spiced meat drifted up from the kitchen. Maybe she'd announce at dinner that she'd decided to become a gluten-free vegetarian. Her family's reaction would at least offer a respite from the tedium that was weighing her down. Except she found herself salivating in response to the savory smells and bread was her favorite food in the world. She'd save her announcement for the next time she was bored.

Pull out of it, Candace told herself. Stop focusing on the negative and think positively. But how? She liked games and puzzles, maybe she could create a game that would bring her out of her funk. Take each one of the five senses, she thought, and list five things in each category that made the holidays special to her. Corny, maybe, but at least it would pass the time until dinner. She grabbed the journal she kept on her nightstand and a pen and got to work.

Smells would be the easiest and Candace would start with that. Gingerbread cookies baking in the oven. The clove-scented candle. The scent of fresh pine whenever she entered the living room where the Christmas tree stood. Wood burning in the fireplace. And the stale air of the local mall crowded with last-minute shoppers.

Sight. This would be a little harder. Twinkling lights on the bushes outside. Presents wrapped in colorful papers of a dozen different designs. The dining table on Christmas Eve, with green boughs in the center, tall beeswax candles, and Great Grandma's fancy china that only came out once a year. The ice skate ornament she got when she was three hanging from the tree. Lily's smile when she woke up on Christmas morning.

Touch next. The heavy, gray, fuzzy wool blanket her dad would bring out just for her every winter. The crunch of snow under her boots when she walked outside. The wall of heat that hit her cheeks when she went back inside after playing in the snow. The rough grip of the toboggan rope as she pulled it up the hill. The silky ribbon slipping through her fingers as she tied a perfect bow on a gift.

Hearing. The jingle of bells on every street corner. The first notes of her favorite carol sung by the church choir. Laughter as they opened their gifts. The crackle of wood burning—she already used the fire, can she do it again? She'd allow it, she decided. Her game, her rules. The sound scissors make when they rip through wrapping paper.

And finally, taste. Maybe this is the easiest one of all, Candace thought, so she needed to make it harder by only picking her absolute favorites. The top five, the pinnacle that make her taste buds dance. From bottom to top. Number five, the first taste of eggnog for the season, especially when Dad grates fresh nutmeg on top. Number four, candy canes. Any other time of the year that fake peppermint taste wouldn't make the list, but it's a Christmas tradition. Number three, the hot, cheesy double-baked potatoes that always made the table for Christmas Eve even when they didn't go with anything else that was being served. Number two, the raw sugar cookie dough she snuck into her mouth while they were cutting it into the shapes of stars, snowmen, and sleighs. It was always way better than after it was baked.

But what about the number one taste? The thing that makes the holidays the holidays, that she doesn't experience the rest of the year. Candace closed her eyes, deep in thought. Far from helping her concentrate, though, shutting out the world around her made her drowsy. Stay awake, her brain told her, you need to finish the last item on the last list. It was the final thought she had before drifting into a deep sleep.

Two

The Assignment

"I'd probably go with hot cocoa on a frigid night such as this," came a voice from nearby, "especially after the special ingredient is added. Or maybe the musky smell of a team of reindeer in the barn as they ready themselves for their annual flight. But that's just me. I'm sure you'll come up with your own top choice."

Candace was groggy and confused as she slowly and reluctantly reentered a state of wakefulness. She didn't recognize the voice. As far as she knew the only males in the house were Dad and Parker, and the blizzard made it unlikely that a visitor had just dropped by. Also, why would a stranger be in her bedroom? Nervously she opened her eyes.

She immediately squawked. This wasn't her bedroom. It wasn't even a room she'd ever seen before. She was lying under a heavy quilt adorned with blue and white snowflakes. The bed itself had a sturdy wooden frame and an intricately carved headboard and footboard with a canopy rising almost to the ceiling. The rest of the room was decorated in a Nordic theme with wood paneling, pictures of wintry scenes on the walls, and colorful blankets draped over every chair. The side table next to the bed had fresh flowers in a vase next to a tray with an assortment of cookies. Light shining from sconces on the walls cast the room in a golden glow. Candace shook her head and blinked several times, expecting to find herself back in familiar surroundings, but the scenery remained unchanged.

"It's about time you woke up," the man said. "There's much to do and very little time." Following the deep sound of the voice, Candace finally noticed an old man across the room, dwarfing the chair he sat in with his rotund belly and broad shoulders. His hair was shockingly white and his matching beard was bushy and full. He wore what appeared to be red ski pants held up by a pair of suspenders and shiny black boots that reflected the room around him. His cheeks were what could only be described as rosy red.

"I'm dreaming," Candace said to herself. "I have to be. But it seems so real."

"This isn't a dream, Candace," the man said sternly. "I only wish it was. You have questions and I'll do my best to answer them quickly. Yes, I'm Santa Claus and you're at the North Pole. No time to get into the specifics about how that happened, but only minutes ago I discovered that I needed someone with your qualifications—smart and creative with the youthful ability to believe what you see and feel despite logic telling you otherwise—and you happened to be the first candidate I found who was asleep, which is critical in getting you here.

"I'm recruiting you for a very specific task," he continued. "Something very meaningful to me has been stolen and you're going to find it and bring it back here for me. Today's Christmas Eve at," Santa consulted the ancient grandfather clock along the wall, "10:22 a.m. North Pole time. That gives you seven hours and thirty-eight minutes to retrieve this object before I need to start my rounds. What do you say, can you do it?"

"Um," Candace stammered.

"Good. Follow me." Santa turned and exited the bedroom door swiftly for a man of his size and Candace had to scramble to untangle herself from the bedspread to catch up. She followed him as he rushed down the hallway and down a flight of stairs, pausing only when he reached the front door that was so thick it looked like it would take both of them to open it. Surprisingly, Santa easily pulled it back, only to be met by a brisk, cold wind. He immediately closed the door.

"You're going to need these," he said, handing Candace a thick woolen overcoat, even thicker mittens with a reindeer design sewn in, and a hat with fur-lined ear flaps. She was still zipping up the coat when Santa reopened the door and stepped out. Candace quickly followed suit.

What greeted her eyes was nothing short of spectacular. A fir tree three stories high sat in the middle of a square, trimmed with thousands of lights in dozens of colors, ornaments that seemed to come alive when she focused on them, and a brilliant sparkling star on the top. Piles of gift-wrapped boxes in a multitude of sizes and shapes surrounded the base of the tree. All around the square were wooden chalet-style structures, music emanating from each one. As Candace jogged after Santa, on her left she passed a long building with wide windows that revealed an enormous building the size of three soccer fields, a flurry of small men and women busy at workstations gluing, painting, and assembling toys of every description. "Elves," she thought to herself.

"Yes, and obviously it's crunch time and they've got their own jobs to do," Santa said to her. "So they can't be of any assistance to you. You'll be on your own. Ah, here we are."

Unlike the neat wooden exteriors of the other buildings they'd passed, the boards for this one were askew, with gaps between them. Hidden in the shadows and invisible to anyone not looking for it stood a black door almost as wide as it was tall and secured by a large metal lock the size of one of Candace's mittens. Santa pulled a silver key ten inches long out of an invisible pocket and within seconds they were inside.

The interior was no more impressive than the outside. There was a single room, long and narrow, with a table in the center stretching nearly its entire length. It was cluttered with strange pieces of equipment, hundreds of unfinished projects, and small piles of sawdust that spilled onto the floor. Each wall contained shelves stacked to the ceiling, each shelf jammed full of toys and other objects. At the far end of the room stood another tall Christmas tree, fully decorated and filling the room with the fragrance of pine. At its peak an ornament shaped in the image of a fairy was barely visible from ground level. Candace stood immobile just inside the door, her jaw dropped open, as she tried to take in all of what the room contained.

"My own private workshop," Santa said softly. "Where I come when I need some time to myself. You're privileged to be invited inside; no one here at the North Pole is allowed in, not even Mrs. Claus. I doubt the elves even know this room exists. What you see is the result of centuries worth of tinkering, which helps me let my thoughts wander and eases my mind. Nothing I work on in here ever leaves this room. Obviously, from all the partially completed pieces you see around you, the process of working has been more important than actually producing a finished project. But in their own way, everything in here has special meaning. One thing especially, more than all the others. And just this morning, I saw that it was gone."

Santa led Candace further into the room, maneuvering around tools and pieces of wood blocking their way before stopping almost halfway down. He reached under the table and pulled out a rickety step stool, dragging it next to one of the shelves. Instinctively, Candace stepped onto it and climbed upward. On the third shelf up, between a duck pull toy missing a wheel and a dollhouse with no doll, was an empty space. A tiny rectangular outline sat in the center of the dusty shelf.

"It's a small box, as you can see," Santa told her, his voice tinged with sadness. "About two inches high with a carving of a sprig of mistletoe on the lid. The box itself is special enough, but it's what's inside that means the most. You don't need to know what that is for now, just find the box. Please don't open it before you hand it to me.

"I need to go now. Preparations, you know. Find this box for me, Candace. I'm counting on you. I'll see you tonight."

Three

Sprig

Candace stood dumbfounded as she watched Santa exit his workshop. Twenty minutes ago she was lying in her own bed trying to find her holiday spirit. Suddenly she's in a strange room at the North Pole thirty seconds after being given an impossible mission from Santa Claus himself. Maybe. Part of her was still convinced that this was an extremely realistic dream and that she'd wake up at any moment. In the end, though, it didn't really matter. Dream or not, what else was she going to do? She'd do her best to track down his box until either she found it or woke up.

But how? She had no idea where to start. The only clue she was given was an empty space on a dusty shelf. It was a safe assumption that whoever took the box didn't hide it in this room and was far away by now. She didn't know the area, had no idea how she'd get around, and everyone up here was so focused on last-minute preparations for Santa's big night that there was no one she could ask for help. Candace used the stool to once again peek at the scene of the crime but, seeing nothing new, climbed back down and leaned against the table, frustrated and near tears.

She sensed more than saw movement from the direction of the Christmas tree. Turning, her eyes were drawn to the ornamental fairy tree topper that graced its peak. She could have sworn that the fairy was moving, as if struggling to escape from its perch, but of course that was ridiculous. As she continued to focus on the fairy ornament, the treetop exploded in a blaze of bright white light, blinding Candace and forcing her to turn her head away. When she looked back, a small luminescent orb was gliding gracefully in her direction. Only when it was near did she make out the figure of a young woman with wings that glowed as she descended.

The fairy was small, maybe six or seven inches tall, but otherwise the perfect image of a person ten times her size. She wore a sparkling green dress with red and gold trim resembling ribbon used to wrap gifts. Her hair at first appeared blonde, but with each small movement it changed color, as if each strand came from a different part of a rainbow. Red, green, blue, yellow, and every combination of the same. Sometimes all of them at once. She hovered a short distance from Candace's eyes, a quizzical look on her face. Neither girl spoke for a minute or more until Candace concluded that the fairy was waiting for her to be the first to introduce herself.

"I'm Candace," she started hesitantly. "I'm not from here and I'm kind of lost and I'm supposed to do something I don't know how to do and I'm scared and really freaked out that I'm talking to a fairy right now. What's your name?"

The creature giggled. "Do you think they give names to tree ornaments here? Even for the North Pole that's a bit extreme. But you'll want something to call me if we're going to work this puzzle together, won't you? Let me see..." The fairy looked around the workshop before pausing when her eyes landed on a clump of leaves tied in a red ribbon hanging from a rafter. "Hmm, maybe 'Misty,' short for 'Mistletoe?' No, too obvious. Fae? No, too redundant." Her eyes went back to the mistletoe. "I know, call me 'Sprig.'"

Candace smiled. "Fine, 'Sprig' it is. I like it. Wait, did you just say we're going to work together on finding the box?"

"Unless you don't want my help," Sprig answered. Candace vigorously shook her head. "Okay, then I'm all in. What do we know so far?"

"Nothing," Candace said sadly. "Well, not exactly nothing. Santa owns a small box with a carving of mistletoe on its lid that's disappeared, and we need to find it before he leaves tonight. The only clue is that yesterday it was on that shelf and now it's not."

"Not exactly the only clue," Sprig said. "Look closer. What do you see on the shelf where the box sat, which you'll also find on the shelf below it, with even more of it on the floor at your feet? Besides dust. I swear, Mrs. Claus really needs to get Santa a dustpan for Christmas."

Candace brought her face closer to the shelves before dropping to her hands and knees to examine the floor. "Crumbs," she said.

"Precisely!" Sprig shouted happily. "Now, do you have a small bag to save them in before the mice devour them? Once you've secured them, we'll take a closer look."

Candace shook her head in despair and stuck her hands deep into the pockets of the coat Santa gave her, only to have her fingers strike plastic. She pulled out a handful of tiny plastic bags that sealed shut by pressing the opening together.

"Perfect!" Sprig said. "Get as much as you can."

Candace was able to fill one of the bags almost to the top. She held it up to the light as she and Sprig examined its contents.

"They just look like cookie crumbs," Candace said. "Santa was probably having a snack."

"Not so," Sprig replied. "There's an advantage to spending all day stuck at the top of that tree. There's not much to do except observe anything that happens here. First, I can tell you that Santa doesn't allow anyone else in here. Second, I've never known him to bring any food or drink in here either. This is kind of a special spot for him reserved for tinkering and thinkering, not eating. So we know it wasn't him that left the crumbs. It has to be the culprit."

"Wait," Candace objected. "If you've had a perfect view of the workshop, didn't you see who took the box?"

"Not if it was dark in here," Sprig said. "Our night vision is no better than yours, and even fairies need to sleep sometime. Can you show me that bag again? I think I noticed something that you didn't because it's probably undetectable to the human eye. Ah, I was right. The crumbs contain a crystal so microscopic that it takes tiny eyes to see them, and even I almost missed them. Can you open up the bag so that I can smell?"

Candace complied, smelling nothing herself. Sprig, though, seemed ecstatic. "Just as I thought. The crumbs contain glop. A very rare spice, very scarce. And never found here at the North Pole. Mrs. Claus would never use it in her baking."

Candace caught on to the excitement in Sprig's voice. "You know where to look next, don't you?" she asked.

"Not precisely, although I know where we need to go to search for our starting point. But there's a stop we need to make along the way."

"I still think 'Fae' is a better name," Candace said.

"And when do I...I mean when does Lily come in?" Lily whined.

"Will there be other dimensions or are we stuck at the North Pole the whole time?" Parker asked.

"Patience," Dad answered. "Patience."

Four

A Surprise Meeting

"Stand still," Sprig commanded. Candace did her best to do so but couldn't stop shivering from the cold. She was standing ankle-deep in snow just outside Santa's workshop watching Sprig rapidly move about in circles, mumbling words that Candace didn't understand. Suddenly the fairy stopped, hovering directly above Candace's head. "Don't move," Sprig reminded her.

Gradually a glittering sheen descended before Candace's eyes, fully encasing both of them in a giant transparent bubble. A gust of wind sent them airborne until the lights of the buildings below faded away as they floated in whichever direction the wind was sending them.

"Where are we going?" Candace asked.

"With luck, where I want us to go," Sprig replied. "Otherwise, wherever the breeze takes us."

With no room to pace, Candace was forced to grit her teeth and fret as the bubble swayed first one way and then another as it traveled through the air. Snowflakes danced and swirled outside the bubble, blocking her sight, so she had no idea where they were or how far up from the ground they were traveling. Her thoughts had just turned to how much time they were burning through when with a "pop" the bubble burst. Candace panicked as she began to fall from the sky, but a split second later she landed in a large snowbank with a resounding "plop."

"We're here, wherever 'here' is," Sprig said as she flew into view. "In this blizzard, we could be anywhere, but let's keep a good thought. Use your instincts and choose a direction to go."

Candace closed her eyes, spun herself around until she was dizzy, and pointed in a random direction.

"As good as any," Sprig said as she began to fly in the chosen route. "Stay close. In this weather, I'll be hard to see."

Candace trudged through the snow, pulling her coat close around her. Eventually she tucked Sprig inside it, as the poor fairy couldn't make any headway against the wind. The pair walked and stumbled, stumbled and walked, for what seemed like hours, but in reality was less than ten minutes, before shadowy outlines of buildings appeared through the haze.

Sprig uttered a frozen cheer and Candace doubled her speed, happily anticipating getting inside and out of the cold. As they got nearer, though, Candace realized her mistake.

These weren't normal buildings, at least in her world. They were thousands of tiny homes hung like birdhouses from trees or stacked into tall skyscrapers. Each one was different from the next, the designs and color combinations only limited by the boundaries of their owners' imaginations.

"Well done, Candace," Sprig said. "When in doubt, follow your gut. Or in your case twirl around until you almost pass out. In any event, now that we're sheltered from the wind, you can free me from the warmth of your coat and stick close. It won't be long. Eighty-three seconds as the fairy flies."

Exactly eighty-three seconds later, Candace followed Sprig through a narrow passage carved into a sheet of rock that rose high above them. Instead of homes, every structure here resembled a pocket-sized office building or business park. There was even a miniature shopping mall that was abuzz with activity. Sprig bypassed them all until she approached a tall, grand tower that gave off an aura of someplace important. As if they were expected, a small door opened and Sprig flew inside, leaving Candace alone.

It wasn't long before Sprig reappeared and signaled Candace to follow her as she continued deeper into the cave. The passage narrowed and the light grew dimmer with each step until Candace couldn't see her feet as she carefully walked on, pressing her hands against the stone walls on either side of her for balance. As they turned a corner, though, she was again blinded by a wall of light. Once her eyes adjusted, she was stunned by what she saw.

It was an exact replica of the bedroom she'd woken up in at the North Pole, down to the carvings on the bedstand and colors of the blankets draped over the chairs. The only differences were the fact that Santa Claus wasn't there, and instead of Candace, nearly buried under the snowflake covers atop the bed, she saw the back of the head of a young girl of around six years old. Candace approached the sleeping girl cautiously, sitting on the edge as she gently shook the girl's shoulder.

The girl sat up and opened her sleepy eyes, saw Candace, and immediately both girls let out a small shriek. The younger girl's first reaction was to hide beneath the blanket, peeking out once only to retreat before finally convincing herself that the scene before her was real.

"Candace, is that really you?" she finally said. "What are you doing here? And where am I? And who is that? What is that?"

Candace took a moment to overcome her surprise but eventually found her voice. "Yes, it's really me. This is my friend Sprig. She's a fairy. Sprig, this is my sister Lily. As far as where we are, I couldn't tell you, but it seems to be some sort of fairyland. Did you just get here?"

Lily nodded. "The last thing I remember is Daddy tucking me in and telling me to have sweet dreams. And I guess I am. This is a dream, isn't it?"

"I'm not sure," Candace replied. "If it is, we're each

having the same dream. A little while ago I woke up at the North Pole in a room just like this with Santa at my bedside. I'm supposed to be on a sort of mission for him and..." She turned to face the fairy. "Sprig, why did we come here?"

Sprig shrugged her shoulders. "No idea, it was just a feeling I had. A very strong feeling I couldn't ignore. I assume it has something to do with her." She pointed at Lily. "But there's no time to waste. We need to get to our next destination, to follow our only clue."

Sprig left the girls and flew away, pausing to look back when she reached the room's exit. "Well, are the two of you coming or am I going to do this by myself?"

As if those were the magic words she'd been waiting to hear, Lily hopped out of bed, finding a pair of boots waiting for her on the floor and a coat and mittens matching Candace's in the closet. Candace watched Lily ready herself. As pleased as she was to have company on her quest, she also felt annoyed that it came in the form of her little sister. How much help could a six-year-old be, she wondered. It's more likely she'll be a burden that'll hold her back from finding the box.

"I'm ready," Lily said once she was dressed. She looked up at Candace and reached for her hand. "But I don't know what I'm ready for. Will you tell me as we go? I'm really confused right now."

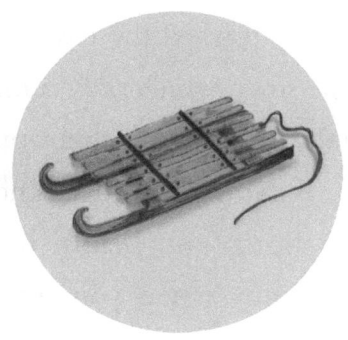

Five

The Town of No Name

"Bundle up," Sprig told the girls as they prepared to leave the cave. "The next part of the journey involves a very cold ride down a steep hill. Expect lots of snow to be sprayed in our faces."

"Why can't we use another magic bubble?" Candace asked. "It was warm in there and protected us from the weather."

"We don't know why, but those bubbles only seem to work in one direction," Sprig replied sadly. "They're not bad at finding the land of fairies, working about half the time, but can't be relied on at all the other way. We'd be just as likely to end up at the South Pole as where we need to go."

"And where do we need to go?" Lily asked. Candace had filled her in on their quest as well as she could while they were making their way toward the cave's exit. It didn't take long to tell the whole story, which only reminded Candace of how little she actually knew about their mission.

"To the 'Town of No Name,' also known as the 'Town of Many Names,'" Sprig said before wrinkling her brow. "Which is kind of funny when you think about how the opposite names each kind of say the same thing. People call it pretty much anything that comes to mind when it becomes the topic of conversation. I've heard it called 'That Place Down There,' 'The Bottom of the Hill Where Odd People Live,' 'You Know Where I Mean,' and at least a hundred more. That's why we say it doesn't have a name but also too many names. Because no name ever sticks and people are always coming up with new ones. Ah, here we are."

They'd arrived at a corral of sorts, with sleds and toboggans of every variety piled up high and sorted by size and descriptions of how well they perform under different conditions. "Lily," Sprig said, "bend down and try to make a snowball, then tell me how you did."

Lily complied, pushing a large handful of snow between her mittens only to have it break apart and fall to the ground. After several attempts, she gave up.

"Would you say 'dry and flaky,' then?" Sprig asked her. Without waiting for an answer she fluttered down the aisle before stopping to read a tag. "One of these will do. A combination of hickory and white oak. Might be a little too fast and harder to steer than one with metal runners, but it's a straight shot down the hill and every second counts. Candace, can you grab that green two-seater?"

Candace complied and dragged it out of the pen by its rope. By that time, the snow was coming down so heavily she couldn't see six inches past her face. She reached out to feel for Lily's hand as Sprig nestled inside her coat once more. "Take eleven giant steps straight forward," Spring instructed her, waiting until she'd done so to continue, "now turn right and take eleven and only eleven baby steps. Good. Help Lily into the front half of the sled then nestle in behind her and wrap her in your legs. Might be a good idea to strap yourselves in. Ready? Both of you lean forward."

No sooner had they leaned forward a few inches than the front of the sled tilted downward and suddenly took off as if it had been pushed. Candace screamed and grabbed Lily tight as they careened down the hill at lightning speed with snow swirling all around them and blocking their sight. Shadows of trees flew by and twice they hit a bump which threw them into the air. Just when they didn't think they could be any more frightened, they felt the sled climb up at an angle as it turned to the left. Candace couldn't imagine how she didn't fall out of the sled as her body pushed against the straps holding them in. If anything, the sled moved even faster coming out of the turn. Two or three terrifying minutes later, the ground leveled off and the sled gradually began to slow, although it was still another ninety seconds before it finally came to a stop.

Candace hadn't realized that somewhere along the way she'd closed her eyes. When she opened them, she saw that they were resting outside the entrance to a sled corral just like the one at the top of the hill. Snow was still falling but coming down lighter here. She could see a street laid out before her and buildings with smoky chimneys off in the distance. Sprig pulled herself out of the confines of Candace's coat.

"Pretty easy run this time, thank goodness," she remarked. "Girls, please put the sled away where it belongs. We need to find the spice shop."

"Do you know the name of the shop?" Candace asked as they trudged in the direction of the town.

"Oh, none of the businesses here have names," Sprig replied. "The people who live here simply know where to go to get whatever it is they need so there's no need for names, and if there aren't any names, there's no need for signs. Not very helpful for outsiders, but then this place doesn't get many visitors. Any at all, really. In our case, if we're going to find the spice shop, we need to follow our noses."

It was Lily who first picked up the scent. "I smell cinnamon!" she cried out. "And... and... what is it? Daddy uses it in cookies he makes at Christmastime."

"Ginger, cloves, and nutmeg, I'm guessing," Candace said. "Now I smell them too. The scent is getting stronger as we keep walking this way. No, wait. I think we need to turn here."

The trio turned down a narrow, crooked side street with barely enough room for Lily and Candace to walk side by side, as small shops pushed up against the edges of their path and squeezed them together. The scent of spice was now so overwhelming that they slowed to peer into each window they passed to see what wares were being sold. Wood carvings, bird cages, warm scarves, ornate ornaments. They began to get discouraged until Sprig squeaked in happiness as they stood outside what appeared to be a rundown shack ready to topple over with the next burst of wind.

"You found it?" both girls asked together.

"I'm sorry, I don't know. I just noticed that this place has a separate entrance for fairies, which brought me joy. I'll be right back." Built high up into the thick door was a miniature opening with flaps, through which Sprig quickly disappeared.

The wait for her to return was brutal. Eventually the tiny door slowly creaked open, casting light from within. Despite their need to get warm, the two girls remained immobile.

Sprig's voice snapped them back to attention. "What are you waiting for?" she said. "Come on in. This is it."

Six

The Spice Shop and Another Surprise

The instant they walked through the door their senses were overwhelmed with the sights and smells of the shop. The first thing to hit them was the confusing scent of an infinite number of spices competing for supremacy of the air. It was impossible to pinpoint a single one, for as soon as Candace was almost ready to identify what she was smelling, the scent dissipated and another one took its place. Before long the aroma of hundreds of spices blended together to fill her nose. Next was the sight of piles of barrels of all sizes and shapes stacked one on top of another reaching from the floor to the ceiling far above, each one overflowing with a colorful spice, with more barrels weighing down overburdened shelves on every wall.

Behind a counter on a tall stool sat a gnarly old gnome, his grizzled gray face sporting an equally gray beard that fell just past his knees. He wore a red striped shirt under a pair of the brightest blue overalls Candace had ever seen. Most striking of all, though, was the red Santa hat with white trim that would have been normal had they been at the North Pole. Candace couldn't stop staring.

Sprig read her mind. "Santa didn't invent that style of hat, you know. It's been popular in these parts for centuries before he started making his rounds. He was just following fashion. Now, don't waste any more time. Isn't there something you want to ask this gentleman?"

"I do!" Lily interjected. "I'll do it. It's my turn." After loudly volunteering, though, she fell silent. "Um, what am I supposed to ask again? I forgot."

Candace dug into her pocket and pulled out the bag of cookie crumbs, handing it to Lily. "Ask him if he recognizes what spices are in this cookie." She lifted Lily up even with the counter in order to ask her question face to face with the shopkeeper.

"Excuse me Mr. Spice Man," Lily said, placing the bag down in front of the man, "can you tell us what's in this cookie?" She stopped speaking until Candace nudged her. "Please."

The man grunted and eyed the group suspiciously, but curiosity overcame him and he reached for the bag with short, gnarled hands. His luminous green eyes were narrow slits as he brought the bag to his nose, but instantly flew open wide as he inhaled.

"Where did you get these?" he snarled. "What kind of treachery is this? Who are you?"

"Please sir," Candace said quickly as she lowered Lily back down to the floor. "We've been tasked by Santa to find an object that was taken from him, probably by someone who was eating these cookies when they snatched it. Sprig here tells us that they contained a special spice and that you might remember who purchased it from you. Please, it's our only lead."

The man glanced at Sprig, who nodded her head. "Glop," he said. "Very rare. I believe I'm the only dealer who has any." He leaned back, stroking his beard. "Haven't sold any in many years. Very expensive you know, but let me check something."

Coming out from behind the counter, Candace was surprised to see that he was barely three feet tall. He pulled a tall ladder from a darkened corner and dragged it to the opposite wall. Climbing up over their heads, he reached for a barrel labeled as cardamom, but instead of pulling off the top he tapped the base in a pattern of three knocks, then two, then three more, springing open a small hidden drawer. He growled in anger.

"Sure enough, someone's dipped into my supply," he told the group. "Stolen it, they did. I need to think." He climbed back down, replaced the ladder, and crawled back up onto his stool. Precious minutes ticked by as he was lost in thought. He opened his eyes with a sigh.

"I know all of my regular customers and it wouldn't be any of them," he said, "so it had to be a stranger. Other than yourselves, the only person it could be was a creature of some sort that stopped by earlier this week. Wore a long golden cloak that hung to the ground with a hood that reached so far around its head that I couldn't see its face. Asked me for something I store in the back room, so I had to leave it alone for five minutes or so. When I got back it was gone. Didn't think much of it at the time but I'll bet it's the thing you're looking for."

"Is there anything else that you can tell us about it? Do you have any idea where it would have gone from here?" Candace was frustrated. She needed something, anything to hold onto, to give her hope.

"Now that I think about it, the creature was carrying a book. I only noticed it because of its size and age. It was very large and very old. Maybe a thousand years or more. And it had a silver and red binding. Of course, everything around here is old, so that may not mean anything. You might want to ask the librarian if anyone's checked out a book of that description."

"Thank you, sir," Sprig said. "Can you point us in the right direction?"

The old man nodded. "Walk in the direction of the ringing bell. When you feel that your noses are as frozen as they can get, enter the first door you see with a holly branch and three berries above the entrance. Oh, and take this with you." He handed them a small, green, sealed bag. "Cocoa from my private stock," he said. "For luck."

The group thanked him profusely and, with some reluctance, headed back out into the cold. They stopped just outside the door and stood still, listening.

"There! Did you hear that?" Lily shouted. "A bell. But I'm not sure where the sound is coming from. Maybe that way?" She pointed to her right. Just as she did so, another chime filled the air. This time all three heard it. They began trudging in the direction Lily had pointed.

As they walked, Candace began glancing behind them every few steps. Sprig was the first to notice. "What are you doing?" she asked from inside Candace's jacket.

"I'm not sure, but I think we're being followed. I don't see or hear anything, it's just a feeling."

"Remember, you have to follow your instincts," Sprig replied. "Tell you what. If there's someone or something back there, they probably haven't seen me and don't know that I'm with you. Let me fly high up and wait to see what I can see while you keep going."

A few minutes later, Sprig returned. "You were right," she said. "A boy, I believe. Whoever it is, he's wearing a coat just like yours. Right now he's hiding in the shadows of the tree we just passed and can't see us. Let's conceal ourselves and wait."

Candace tucked Sprig back inside her coat as she and Lily sprinted off to the side and pressed themselves against the side of a building, trying their best to blend in. A minute later a tall figure emerged in their line of sight, stopping and looking around as if he lost something.

"Now!" Candace shouted, and she and Lily ran toward the figure. As they got close, both girls slipped on the snow and slid several feet directly into the boy's knees, knocking him to the ground.

"Hey!" he said in a deep voice. "That wasn't nice."

"Neither is following us," Candace said in a huff as she wiped snow off her eyes. "And it's creepy. Who are you and what do you want?"

"Should I be offended that you don't recognize my voice?" the boy said as he stood and faced the girls. "We've only lived together for your whole lives."

"Parker!" Lily said as she gave him a big hug.

"Parker?" Candace said with much less enthusiasm. "What are you doing here, and why are you following us? The fact that you're our brother doesn't make it any less creepy."

"Santa asked me to keep tabs on you," Parker explained. "He told me you were on some sort of dangerous mission and wanted me to make sure you don't get into any trouble."

"How come everyone gets to meet Santa but me?" Lily whined before pulling herself back on track. "Do you want to help us?"

"I guess continuing to follow you no longer makes sense," Parker said. "And I was feeling left out anyway. Is it okay to join you? That way if you do get into trouble, I'll know right away."

Candace took her time to respond as she looked at her brother and tried to decide if she could trust him. He was dressed in an identical coat, hat, and scarf that made him look like her twin. He must be telling the truth, she thought, if Santa loaned him the same clothing. Even though he was a few years older than she was, though, she still wasn't sure if he would be of any help with their quest. Older brothers as a general rule are useless, she thought. Had she been able to read Parker's own thoughts at that very moment, she'd have discovered he was thinking the same thing about younger sisters.

"The more the merrier, I guess," she finally said reluctantly. "We're following the sound of the bell until our noses are ready to fall off or some such nonsense. Parker, the fairy hovering near me is Sprig. Come along, we don't have time for a drawn-out family reunion."

The four travelers moved forward slowly against the wind, with each step feeling colder. They began to lose feeling in their fingers and toes but moved on as the sound of the bell gradually became louder. Suddenly, Lily stopped.

"My nose!" she cried. "It's frozen!"

"Mine too," Candace added. "It got so much worse in the last two steps. This must be what the spice man meant. Lily and I will take this side of the street. Parker, go with Sprig on that side. We're looking for a door with a holly branch and three berries on it overhead."

They called out the numbers of berries as they counted. Five, one, eight, none. With every step they felt their noses getting even more frozen. Finally, Parker and Sprig shouted together. "Three!"

Candace and Lily hurried to their side as Parker turned the doorknob. Nothing. It wouldn't budge. Candace tried, Lily tried. No movement. Only when they all turned it together and leaned on the door did it give way. They tumbled through the door and landed in a heap. They didn't care if this was the right place or not. It was warm in here.

"Shhh," they heard from several directions as they noisily scrambled to their feet. "Yep," thought Candace. "We're in a library."

Seven

The Library

The group instantly hushed themselves and looked around to take in their surroundings. In some ways the room they were in looked like that of any other library. Shelves lined with books, patrons studying at tables, and a librarian settled behind a desk. However, that was where the similarities ended. From the outside, the building had the appearance of every other small, run-down shack they'd been passing since entering the town. Inside, though, was another story.

For one, the atrium in which they stood was impossibly tall. Candace counted at least seven levels rising above them before darkness hid what may have been even more. As far as the eye could see books were crammed onto shelves that touched the ceilings and extended out to the very edges of each floor. Instead of the usual step stool to reach the upper shelves, though, each one had a narrow walkway with tiny stairs linking each level. The group watched in wonder as small gnomes roamed the walks, pulling out books no bigger than a postcard before perusing them and either tucking them under their arms or shoving them back between the other books.

As they stared and gazed upward, the four adventurers shuffled in unison toward the librarian's desk, where Candace and Lily gave a quiet gasp. Behind the desk on a tall chair sat a woman who was nearly a carbon copy of the man at the spice shop. No more than three feet tall and probably a handful of inches shorter, the woman shared his gnarled look, bright green eyes, worn complexion, and voluminous gray hair falling below her knees in place of the beard. She even wore the same red striped shirt and overalls, with a Santa hat perched upon her head.

"Can I help you?" she growled in a tone implying that assisting them was the last thing she wanted to do.

"We're here to ask about a book, or more particularly about the person or thing that may have checked out a book," Candace replied before briefly explaining their mission for Santa and what brought them to the library, including a description of the book.

"Hmm," the librarian said before repeating it a second time. "If it came from here and is the size you say it is, it would have to have come from the eleventh floor. Haven't been up there myself for half a lifetime. Might be a bit dusty. Come along."

They followed her across the room under the watchful eyes of everyone there, stopping at the bottom of a narrow rainbow-colored spiral staircase. "Go on, now," she commanded. Tallest one first up five steps, then the next tallest up four, and so on. Pixie, you can hitchhike with whomever you like."

Candace giggled at Sprig's offended expression. She wondered if being called a pixie was an insult to a fairy. She had always thought they meant the same thing, so she'd have to ask later. For now, she kept her amusement to herself.

"Hold on now," the old woman told them. Suddenly the staircase began to move upward, spinning and spiraling as it did so. Lily was confused. It didn't seem like they were going up at all, only turning in circles, but every time she glanced down the ground floor was farther away. After a few minutes, she stopped looking and had to close her eyes and grab onto the handrail. She was getting very, very dizzy.

She wasn't the only one. It must have taken ninety seconds to get to the right floor, and when they stepped off the stairs Candace nearly fell and Parker lurched sideways before bumping into a wall. Only Sprig was unaffected.

"This way," the librarian said. The floor was dark, the only light coming from the main floor far below and an occasional flicker from tiny dim bulbs lining the bookshelves. The librarian was right. Every book was covered in an inch of dust, making it almost impossible to determine where one book ended and its neighbor began. They followed her down aisle after aisle before she halted abruptly, causing Parker to bump into Candace from behind.

"Ah, yes," she said. "This is where it was. It was the only book we had that would have been the right size to fit in this spot. Don't know what good it'll do you to see the empty space where it used to be but you can stay as long as you need to." She handed Parker a flashlight. "Use this. When you're done, go back down using the same stairs we came up on. You can walk down them if you need to." In an instant, she was gone.

Parker shone the light on the shelf. "She's right," he said sadly. "What good is this doing?"

"There's got to be something here, some sort of clue," Candace said. "Otherwise we've failed."

The three stood staring at the shelf in front of them for several minutes without speaking, Parker shining the light around aimlessly. Suddenly he got very still and moved the light across several shelves repeatedly in the same pattern until Candace had to say something.

"Do you see something or are you just being annoying, making random patterns on the books?" she asked.

"I'm not sure," Parker said. "Have you noticed that there are other missing books? Everywhere else around us they're jammed in with no space between them, but all along this one shelf there's a book missing here and there. And the shelf where they sat has no dust, meaning these books were taken out recently. Look."

He was right. For about twenty feet there were several empty spaces, some high up and some down low, but never two in a row. In all there may have been twenty-five or thirty missing books.

"Great," Candace said, "but what does it mean, if anything?"

Parker slowly traced the trail of empty spaces from the left to the right, then went back to do it again and again. After the tenth time, he stopped. "It's a map," he said proudly.

"A map?" Sprig asked. "How?"

"How was I so brilliant or how does it work?" Parker said with a smile. His sisters were not amused. "Candace," he continued, "I see you have a notebook. Start on one end of a page and draw a line from one empty space on the shelf to the next. When the space is higher, go up, and vice versa. Then show us what you drew."

"It does look like a trail," she said as she began to sketch. "It weaves around, perhaps following a street? Maybe it doesn't mean anything, but it's all we've got." Once she finished, she had her three companions check her work and all agreed her drawing followed the spaces with missing books perfectly, and that somehow she'd made it look like a map they could follow.

Energized, the group made its way back to the spiral staircase and slowly descended, stopping at the front desk to thank the librarian.

"Here, take one of these," she said, handing them a long cinnamon stick. "We like to use them as fragrant bookmarks."

Bundled up once more, the group exited the library and

looked in every direction. Candace held out her sketch for all to study.

"There!" Lily cried as she pointed. "See how the sidewalk bends that way? Just like what you drew." She started running in the direction she pointed. Candace and Parker looked at each other, shrugged their shoulders, and started to follow.

"Come along, Pixie," Candace said to Sprig with a giggle. She was lucky she didn't hear the reply.

Eight

Musical Clue

Lily took the lead and held the map while the others followed. Whenever there were multiple options of where to go, which happened frequently, the four consulted the map and confirmed which direction to walk. Over the next ten minutes they turned left, and right, and at one point the path they were on diverged in seven different directions. They quickly realized their first choice there was wrong, forcing them to retrace their steps and consult the map again. The correct path brought them almost in a complete circle, after which Lily stopped walking. With each step they had moved deeper into the depths of the town and she feared they would never find their way back.

"We're almost at the end of the map," Lily told the others. "We just need to turn that corner."

Candace inhaled a big breath. "Are you ready to see where

the map brought us? Any guesses? I'm thinking another shop. Or maybe a hill to sled down."

"It could be an actual person with information," Parker added. "Or if we're lucky the place where the box is hidden."

When they rounded the corner, though, it was nothing any of them had predicted or expected. They found themselves at the edge of a large open square crowded with locals gathered in a tight group watching something. Despite their height advantage, they couldn't see what the crowd was looking at. The faint sound of singing drifted through the frigid air from the far side of the gathering. Joining hands, with Sprig perched on Candace's shoulder, they began making their way into the crowd and slowly moved through to the front with the help of gentle nudges and strategic moves into gaps. As they neared the front, they could see a group of gnomes holding songbooks.

"That explains the singing," Sprig whispered. The choir was no different from any other choir the children had seen, except for the fact that it was comprised of thirty gnomes nearly hidden by the long gray beards and hair of their neighbors and their shimmering gowns that changed color with every burst of wind. Their voices were, to be charitable, similar to what a cat with a bad cold would sound like if it could form words.

The group squatted down and moved to the side to avoid drawing too much attention away from the singers and restlessly listened to two gnome versions of Christmas carols.

"What are we supposed to do?" Candace asked the others in a hushed tone. "Is this a dead end? Did we make a mistake in thinking our sketch was a map?"

Just as she asked her question, a smattering of applause broke out from the audience, which began to scatter. The children felt a rising sense of panic. If they were meant to be here, there must be something they were supposed to do, but what was it?

At that moment one of the choir members stumbled and bumped into Lily, dropping her songbook as she fell. Once Lily recovered, she bent down to pick it up, then turned to return it to the woman. There was no one there.

"That's weird," Parker said. "Maybe she meant to give it to us. Maybe there's another map, or some sort of clue inside. Let's take a look."

"Maybe we could look at it inside somewhere out of the cold and where there's more light," Candace suggested. "Like over there. That looks like a bakery, or a tea shop. Let's give it a try."

It was a tea shop. By now the group was used to the outside of a building bearing no resemblance to what was within, so it was no surprise to push past a broken, squeaky door into a bright colorful room bursting with activity. Wooden tables in purple, yellow, green, and blue surrounded a tall, fat Christmas tree that dominated the center of the room. The tree was a wonder to behold, with what seemed to be miles of strings of lights, ornaments of unique and intriguing designs, and glittering tinsel. Servers in green and red aprons and the standard Santa hats bustled from table to table. One of them gestured to the group to seat themselves at a table.

No sooner did they sit down than the woman brought over a tray of three steaming teapots. Lily's was in the shape of a reindeer, Parker's a Christmas tree, and Candace's a wrapped box complete with a ceramic ribbon and bow. Each was given a matching cup and a miniature version of the reindeer mug was placed near Sprig. The server disappeared briefly before returning with a sleigh-shaped red pitcher of cream, a matching green pitcher of milk, and a bowl of deep golden sugar.

"We don't have money," Candace protested.

"Free for guests of Santa," the gnome replied before hurrying off to another table.

Candace took the lead in pouring the tea while Parker passed the cream and sugar around. The warmth of the sweet tea reinvigorated the tired crew.

"Let's see what's inside that songbook," Parker told Candace. She opened it up to reveal a single page of music with only three measures of what presumably was one of the songs the choir had just sung.

Parker sighed with disappointment. "I guess that shouldn't be a surprise inside a songbook. Sheet music."

"Let me see," Candace said, taking the paper in her hands. She held it up to the light, looking for a hidden message. Nothing. Disappointed, she began humming the tune on the sheet in her hands. Her face grew more confused as she tried to navigate the music.

"This is just weird," she finally announced. "I mean, I'm no expert, but I do play clarinet so I know a little about how music should sound. Even though it's only a short part of a song, it isn't normal. There are combinations of notes here that make no sense and sound terrible together."

Parker brightened immediately. "Musical cryptography," he said proudly.

"What?" Candace answered. "What are you talking about? Speak English." Lily and Sprig looked at each other with puzzled expressions.

"I saw a video on it once," he said. "You know that I study music too, but I also like spy stories. This is both. It's where musical notes are used as a code. It's not as uncommon as you think. Some composers would create a musical code to spell out their name or the name of someone they loved in one of their pieces. Maybe that's what this is. Each note represents a letter of the alphabet."

Partly inspired and partly desperate, the group of four stared at the sheet of music looking for a way to decipher the message, if any. Candace continued to hum the music.

"What are those squiggles?" Lily asked.

"Rests," Candace answered. "Like a break between notes. Or...a break between words. Good job, Lily, I think you're onto something. If true, the message starts with a four-letter word, then a three-letter word, then another four-letter word."

"The most common letter in the English language is 'e,' right?" Parker asked, not waiting for an answer. "See how the same note appears four times out of the eleven letters? What if that's an 'e'? Where it is on the staff might help us with the other letters." He noticed the blank look on Lily's face. "The staff is the lines and spaces with the notes. Where the notes are placed tells the musician which note to play. For example a note in the first space near the bottom is an 'f.' The next one up on the line is a 'g.'"

"And the four notes you think are an 'e' are on the line for an 'f,'" Candace said. "So unless the message has four 'f's out of eleven letters in it, which seems unlikely, these notes don't match up with the letter names of real musical notes. Which makes sense since there are only eight notes on a scale and we need twenty-six letters, one for each letter of the alphabet."

"I don't think whoever did this would make it too complicated, so let's start simple. Some of these notes have sharps and flats—," Parker began.

"And there's no such thing as an F flat on a keyboard—" Candace interrupted.

"So let's assume that each note on a scale corresponds

to a letter of the alphabet, presumably in order," Parker continued. "We can work down the scale from the note that we think is 'e'."

Candace did so out loud. "So if F is 'e,' then F flat—which is nonsense to me—would be 'd,' E sharp is 'c,' E is 'b,' and E flat is 'a.' Now let me go up the scale."

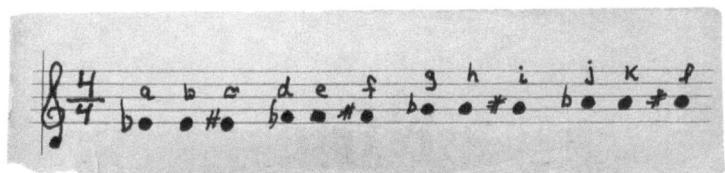

She did so, too slowly for the three watching her. When she finished, all of them raced to decipher the code first by matching the notes with the letters Candace had written on the sheet of music. Candace and Parker tied.

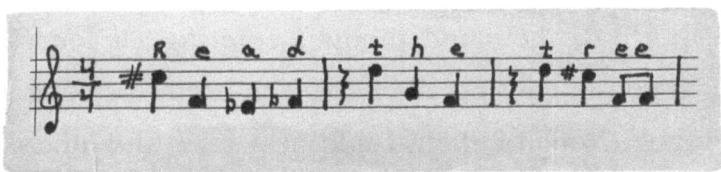

"'Read the tree'? What does that mean?" Parker said dejectedly.

"It's not fair to solve a puzzle and it's another puzzle," Lily said.

"I couldn't agree more," Candance said.

"So where does that leave us?" Sprig asked. For the longest time, no one answered.

Nine

Reading the Tree

The four sat silently sipping their tea, looking absentmindedly in the direction of the tree in the center of the room, hoping an idea would come to them. And then one did, the same thought entering all four minds simultaneously, causing all of them to begin speaking at the same time. None of them could hear what the others were saying over the noise, so eventually they all stopped talking.

"I'll go first," Parker said, "although it's almost too obvious. I can't believe I didn't see it right away. For the longest time I was trying to figure out what "read the tree" means while at the same time I was staring right at that enormous Christmas tree thirty feet away from our table."

"Exactly," Candace said. "What other tree could the message mean? But identifying the tree is only the first step.

If it's the right tree, we're supposed to read it. I've read books and people's expressions and the backs of cereal boxes, but never a tree. I don't know where to start."

The group again fell into silence until Lily began snickering. "Lily," Parker chastised, "this is serious. What do you find to laugh about?"

"Nothing," she replied. "Except when I stare at the tree for a long time my eyes get tired and it gets all fuzzy like when Daddy takes pictures but forgets to focus the camera. Then the red lights on the tree look kind of like the shape of a dinosaur or maybe a reindeer."

Candace, Sprig, and Parker exchanged looks before turning their chairs to directly face the tree, purposely letting their eyes relax until all the distractions in the room disappeared and only the tree remained. After several seconds their sights blurred, with only the red lights shining through their haze, just as Lily had described.

"I see more of a dog," Parker said.

"No, it's a bird, maybe an eagle," Candace said. "But this isn't helping. It's like looking at constellations in the sky. They can be almost anything depending on how you connect the stars."

"Maybe we're overthinking this," Sprig added. "Maybe we're not supposed to find a shape from the lights. It could be something else. Like another code."

"Or another map," Lily said.

"Of course!" Candace and Parker cried in unison. "Let's

go take a closer look," Parker suggested.

When they got to the tree, Sprig flew around it in a circle. "The other side has lights of all the same colors this side does," she said, "except red. Why would that be? I think Lily's right--we need to focus on red lights."

"Every red light is identical to all of the other red lights," Parker said. "There's probably forty of them and they're scattered all over this side of the tree. If it's a map, it's impossible to read. We'd be walking in a dozen different directions."

"Maybe the lights aren't the clues, they're just marking the spot of the clues," Candace said excitedly. "Even though the lights themselves are all the same, is there something that makes some of them different from the others?"

"Ornaments," Lily said. "At least the lights I can see. When we were at the table I wondered why the red lights are the only ones that have ornaments hanging right next to them, almost touching. Not all of them, only some."

"Good catch, Lily," Candace said as she stepped back to get a better view up the tree. "That would narrow it to around ten lights. Sprig, can you fly up and see which of the higher lights have ornaments next to them and I'll sketch the pattern?"

"Wait," Parker interjected. "You also need to tell us what kind of ornaments. Look, the handful we can see down here are all buildings. This one's a church, the one over there's a toy store, and I can see a cabin. None of the other ornaments on the tree that aren't next to red lights are buildings. So if this is a map, what do you want to bet that these ornaments match buildings we'll find along the way?"

"Brilliant!" Candace said. "Sprig, do your thing."

For the next ten minutes, Sprig flew up and hovered next to red lights with an ornament nearby while Candace sketched its location, then came down to describe the ornament before flying to the next red light. When she was finished, the group looked at what Candace had drawn and felt instantly deflated. It was a mess.

"This doesn't look like any map I've ever seen," Candace moaned. "The locations aren't in any sort of pattern to let us know how to travel from one to the next. They're all jumbled and we'd waste time trying to find a church and not even know if it's the right church on the right street. We need to know what order to follow."

"We're missing something," Parker agreed. "And I think I know what it is. When you put tinsel on your Christmas tree, how do you do it?"

"One strand at a time," Candace answered. "So that it's even all over the tree."

"I throw bunches on," Lily said.

"Right," Parker said. "And this tree isn't either of those. The tinsel has been placed strategically. Look, we can clearly see four of the red light ornaments from here. The chapel has three strands of tinsel hanging around it, the toy store seven, the cabin one, and what looks like a coffee shop scene around ten."

"It's the order we go in!" Sprig shouted. "Be right back." Without waiting one more second, she again flew up and down tallying the number of tinsel strands were near each ornament. By the end, all ten had different numbers of strands.

"Excellent," Candace said. "Let's go back to the table and I'll redraw the map."

Starting on a fresh page, Candace drew small images of the structures to match the ornaments, leaving them in the same relative locations as they were on the tree, then drew lines and arrows from one to another starting with the cabin, which had a single strand of tinsel and ending with the coffee shop, which had ten.

"It looks like we're going to get dizzy with all of the different directions this takes us," Parker said. "Hopefully we find streets that match what you just drew."

As they got up to leave, the woman who'd served them approached their table with a red flask. "We don't waste here," she said as she poured the leftover milk and cream from the table into the flask. Parker thanked her and stored it in his coat pocket. The group headed for the door.

Ten

Following the Tinsel Trail

The wind hit them with an icy blast the moment they exited the door. With trembling hands Candace held the crude map out in front of her where the entire group could read it. She pointed to their right.

"Does that look like the right way?" she asked. "On paper the route curves a little bit because the line between the first two points has to bend to go around the back of number six. Does that look like a curve to you?"

"More than the other way," Parker agreed. "Besides, we just came from the left and I don't remember seeing a structure that looks more like a cabin than any of the rest of these shacks. If we're wrong, we can backtrack."

"Let's just move," Lily told the others. "I'm freezing."

As the three children moved forward in a huddle, Sprig

nestled into the folds of Parker's stocking cap in order to stay warm while acting as a lookout to help spot the cabin. And it worked, for she was the first one to see something.

"Look! Over there!" she cried. What she saw was still what Parker would categorize as a shack, but instead of vertical planks, the outer walls were tree trunks placed horizontally in the customary pattern of a log cabin nestled in a forest. Here, though, it sat directly in their path as the walkway they were on split to either side of it.

"Candace," Parker said in a shaky voice. "Can you please unfold the map so that we can see your sketch of the first building?"

Candace could sense in Parker's voice that something was bothering him. "Parker, what is it?" she asked. "What's wrong?"

Instead of answering, Parker simply pointed to her drawing of a cabin and then at the structure in front of them. Candace and Sprig both gasped. The quick sketch she made of the ornament was an identical match to the real thing, down to the number and placement of the windows, the slanting roof, the three steps up to the front porch, and the smoke coming from the chimney.

"That is so weird," Candace said.

"I guess we shouldn't be surprised," Parker said, finding his voice. "Everything about this adventure has been strange."

Parker ran ahead to open the door, but it wouldn't budge. To one side of it, though, sitting on a ledge outside a frosty windowpane, sat three miniature bottles no bigger than their thumbs labeled "maple syrup," with a single strand of tinsel hanging from each one. "They must be meant for us," Parker said as he dropped one into his coat pocket and handed the other two to his sisters. "But now where? What's next on the list?"

"A shop with a candle in the window," Candace replied. "And it looks like we go right again."

"I see a light!" Lily said, pointing down the way Candace suggested. "Everything else is so dark."

The group headed in the direction of the tiny pinpoint of light that Lily had spotted. Above the door of the building was a sign saying "Bookstore." One side of the sign had come away from its bindings so that it was hanging at an angle with a corner of it resting on the top of the door frame. Candace pulled out her drawing, and again her sketch was a perfect match to the bookstore, down to the dangling sign and candle in the window.

"I guess we shouldn't be surprised," Parker said. "Do you think we're meant to go inside this one?"

When he tried opening the door it was locked tight, preventing them from entering. On the ground next to it, though, were three candles, one each in silver, gold, and white with sparkles. Two strands of tinsel were wrapped around each one. Lily grabbed the glittery candle, leaving Parker and Candace to choose between the other two.

At that moment a church bell sounded off in the distance

and the frozen four quickly turned away from the bookstore and followed the sound. The wind had picked up and snow pounded their faces, increasing their misery with each step. By the time they were ten steps away from the chapel doors, their limbs were so cold they could barely move and their strength and will to continue were waning. This time the door gave way when Parker pulled at it, but he struggled to open it far enough to enter and needed Candace's help.

Unlike the tea shop, which shocked them with how large and roomy it was despite a modest exterior, here the inside of the chapel was barely bigger than a bedroom. Stained glass windows not visible from the outside somehow gave off a pale glow, illuminating pews barely big enough for three children and a fairy to rest. They slowly lowered themselves down, squealing with surprise to find that their seats were heated. In fact, the entire room radiated a warmth that instantly brought them back to life and gave them a renewed motivation to continue their journey. Three long strands of tinsel hung from the alter at the front of the church.

"I could stay here for longer, but we can't afford to linger," Candace said. "Let's see what's next." She opened the map. "I guess if anything will inspire us to leave the warmth of this little chapel and move on, it's a candy shop. Shall we go?" With a groan, the group rose to their feet and exited back into the cold.

Their path continued to veer to the right in a subtle curve. A few minutes later a brightly lit storefront appeared, a contrast to the gloom all around them. Even without the large sign identifying it as a sweet shop with four strands of tinsel decorating the lettering, they would have recognized it as an exact duplicate of Candace's drawing on the map.

To their delight, the door opened easily and they stepped inside to the strong aroma of sugar and sweets. They weren't so happy to discover that all the candy was locked tight inside glass cabinets with the exception of four striped candy canes and four chocolate bars sitting on a table in the center of the shop. The candy canes were labeled with a small sign saying "for now" and the chocolate a similar sign stating "for later."

Looking at each other with a shrug of their shoulders and a nod of their heads, they stored the chocolate deep within their coat pockets and took a lick of the candy canes. Immediately a warmth spread through their entire body, radiating to the very tips of their fingers and toes. Each of their faces took on a rosy red glow.

"Wow!" said Lily.

"Just what we needed," Sprig added.

Unfortunately, the candy canes dissolved quickly as they sucked on them and were soon gone. The warmth they provided did at least give them the will to venture back out into the cold, where the weather continued to get worse. On the porch of the next building on the map, an outerwear store, sat three pairs of earmuffs in red, green, and green and red stripe, each wrapped in five strands of tinsel. The children quickly put them on while Sprig burrowed deep inside Candace's coat to warm her icy wings.

The next stop was a post office that was in a shack so worn down that Parker was surprised it was still standing. Again, there was no way inside to warm up, but four colorful Christmas cards with their names on each one awaited them. When they opened the cards, a burst of confetti with six strands of tinsel exploded into the air around them to their great delight.

Building seven was a toy store. Lily was excited when the door easily opened, but when they stepped inside the only toys in sight were three pedal cars lined up one behind the other facing down a long, narrow passageway. Seven strands of tinsel hung from each one. Candace consulted the map. "It does kind of look like our path goes straight through this place," she told the others. Without another word, the children each climbed into a car and pedaled down the hallway until they reached another door.

They opened the door to find themselves back outside in the chill, but immediately across the street stood the eighth building, a bakery. Wonderful, sweet smells drifted in their direction and they lost no time crossing the path and entering. The sight that awaited them inside took their breaths away. Transparent display cases on either side of them stretched the entire length of the room and were filled with pastries of every kind. Donuts, cinnamon rolls, crullers, strudels, sweet rolls filled with jam, eclairs, croissants, and more. Hanging from hooks to one side were four waxy bags and tongs below was a sign saying "One for now, one for later." The sign was framed with eight strands of tinsel, two per side.

"I'm in heaven," Parker sighed. "How can I possibly limit myself to two?"

"Best we follow what the sign says," Candace cautioned. "We don't know what would happen if we don't."

Before long, the four companions were happily wiping sugar off their faces, each one with a bag containing their snack for later. It was with great reluctance they left the bakery. The next stop was a Christmas shop, where a peek in the windows revealed a delightful assortment of ornaments and other decorations, but to the group's disappointment the door was closed tight. All that they found to confirm they were in the right place were nine strands of tinsel hanging from the doorknob along with an ornament painted with a picture of some sort of storefront.

"We have one more to go, the last one," Candace announced as they consulted the map. To their surprise, her sketch of the tenth and final stop was gone and in its place was a replica of the design on the ornament they took from the Christmas shop. Parker held out the ornament as they continued down the path. It displayed a brightly lit, cheerful entranceway with a row of snowmen lining each side of the walkway to the front door. Within minutes, they arrived at a festive shop that matched the one on the ornament perfectly. The sound of carols drifted out from inside. The windows were so caked with snow and ice, they had no idea what they'd find within the doors, provided they could get in at all.

The four gathered in front of the shop, gave each other fateful glances, and nodded their determination to discover what they'd find on the other side of the door. Parker pulled open the door, they marched inside, and then immediately froze still as soon as the door closed behind them. In front of them, in the center of the room, stood a very tall Christmas tree surrounded by a number of colorful tables occupied by groups of gnomes drinking from steaming mugs.

"We're back in the tea shop where we started from," Parker groaned. "We just made a giant circle and came in through a door on the opposite side from where we left."

Eleven

The Mage

The group froze just inside the door of the tea shop, unsure what to do. Moving further inside would make it seem like they were right back where they had been earlier with no progress to show for their trek around the town. But going back outside would leave them in the cold with no idea where to go. As a result, they didn't move, didn't speak, and didn't take any action at all.

After a few long moments, a familiar face approached them. It was the gnome woman who'd served them at their table the first time. "I didn't expect to see you back so soon," she began. "But it's good that you are. She's waiting for you."

"We didn't know we'd be back," Parker grumbled, sounding as annoyed as he felt. "Wait, what did you say? Who's waiting for us? We don't know anyone here."

The woman was unfazed by Parker's interruption. "Shortly after you left someone came asking for you, and she's been waiting ever since. Her presence here has caused quite a stir, as she's been highly revered for centuries in this region but seldom seen. In fact, as old as some of our townspeople are, no one in this town has set eyes on her before, but we knew instantly who she was from the tales. She's known as the Christmas Mage. I don't know her real name. You'll find her sitting in that dark corner at the far end of the room."

"I don't like this," Lily whispered. "She sounds scary."

"I agree," Candace said. "But we don't really have a choice, do we? We have no idea where to go or what to do next and are totally stymied. Then out of nowhere appears a mystical creature waiting for us? It's almost as if we were meant to come back to this shop."

"That doesn't make it any less frightening," Parker added, "but you're right. We have to do this. And Lily, don't worry, there are four of us and only one of her." Which means three of us can get away while she casts a spell on the other one, he thought, but he didn't say it.

Sprig led the way with the three children shuffling slowly behind her, unconsciously stalling with their slow pace. As they walked, though, they each felt drawn forward, as if an unseen force was pulling them in the direction of the corner. All too soon, they reached their destination, where their jaws dropped in shock.

They each had their own image of the mage drawn in their minds from the brief description by the gnome server. They were all different in the details, but what they had in common was that she would be as short as the rest of the gnomes, wrinkled and decrepit with age and witchlike in appearance, with a mean face, jagged teeth, and razor-sharp claws. Instead, the mage was a stunningly beautiful woman, perhaps the most beautiful any of them had ever seen. She was extremely tall as she stood before them, her height accentuated by a pointed hat wrapped with a red ribbon. A burgundy velvet dress lined with a red sash flowed from her shoulders downward to the floor. A brown leather corset held in her waist, tied with wide brown straps.

Most surprising of all, though, were her facial features. She looked barely older than Parker or Candace, her skin smooth and radiant. Lilac-colored hair draped over her shoulders, falling past her waist. Delicate hands with sparkly nails beckoned them to sit. Three chairs had already been lined up opposite where she stood. As the children sat, she lowered herself into her own chair.

"You're so pretty," Lily gushed. "What's your name?"

"I've been called many things across many generations," the woman answered in a gentle voice. "But never by my given name, and I won't mention it here. Besides, there's no time for introductions. We have much to do and your deadline is fast approaching."

"Are you here to help us? To tell us where to go next to find Santa's box?" Candace asked.

"My purpose is unspoken," the mage replied. "All I do is allow unseen forces to work through me and what their intent is, I do not know. What I can tell you is that when you leave here the world around you will not be the same as it is at this moment. That's when you'll need this." As she spoke, the mage reached deep within a pocket hidden among the folds of her skirt, pulling out a small amulet of silver with a shiny red ruby in the center, hanging by a silver chain. The tree lights reflecting off of the ruby surrounded the group with a field of dancing colored lights.

She held out the amulet by its chain, slowly moving it back and forth in front of the children, offering it to each one. Parker and Lily leaned back, away from it. Candace, though, was drawn to it and felt her arm reaching outward without having told it to move, while at the same time the amulet floated out to meet her hand. Not even realizing what she was doing, she clutched it, quickly hanging the chain around her neck.

"It chose you," the mage said, smiling. "Use it well. Now, we must move on to the other reason I am here. Draw yourselves near." Again dipping her hand deep into a pocket, she pulled out a small vial of a clear liquid, then cupped her hands and pushed them together before pulling them apart, revealing two tea cups, which she set on the table. One was painted blue with white snowflakes, the other white with flakes of blue. She tipped the vial from high above the first cup, liquid slowly falling into it in a stream until it was half full. She repeated the gesture with the second cup, restored the vial to the pocket from which it came, then closed her eyes.

She began humming a haunting tune, first slowly but gradually faster and faster. The group watched the liquid in the cups begin to rise into the air in spiral patterns. As it did so, the temperature in the room dropped at an alarming rate, forcing the children to pull their coats close and to don their hats and gloves. They watched, fascinated, as the streams of liquid began to break apart into snowflakes matching the colors of the flakes on the cups. Small flurries began to swirl, growing rapidly in intensity along with the speed of the mage's humming. As they spun, the flurries grew in size until the whole table was immersed in a blinding blizzard of white and blue flakes.

The group could no longer see the mage even though she was right across the table from them, but they heard her quivering voice once the humming stopped. "Trust the snowmen," she said, "all but one."

"What? What does that mean?" Parker shouted through the storm, but he heard no reply. The snow continued to circle around them, the visibility down to inches. The air was as cold as it had been outside. The group huddled together in a circle for warmth, trying to keep their backs to the raging snow and the biting wind which entrapped them. Then suddenly it all stopped, the snow falling away in an instant.

Sprig emerged from within Candace's coat and perched on her shoulder as the three children straightened up. The mage was gone. The whole tea shop was gone. In fact, the entire town with all its shacks and sidewalks and alleys and people was gone. They were standing together in what appeared to be an ice cave, with towers of cold, clear ice rising above them in all directions. Their breath froze as it left their mouths, falling to the slippery floor in a cascade of crystals.

"Whoops," said Parker.

Twelve

Snowmen Show the Way

"We were just magically transported into the middle of a forest of ice and all you can say is 'whoops'"? Candace said testily.

"Given every other thing we've encountered on this day, does what just happened really surprise you?" Parker replied. "There's no sense overreacting. So why don't you stop quibbling over the words I use and help us figure a way out of here?"

"He's right," Sprig said. "We need to work together as a team. Arguing among ourselves does no good. Now, can we assume that we were meant to be brought here, that it's a necessary step to get us to wherever we need to be next? It's possible that this is a good thing." She stopped and looked off to her left. "Lily, what are you doing?"

"If we need to take more steps like you said, I thought it would be easier if we did it on ice skates," Lily said. She was sitting on a ledge of ice, taking off her boots. At her feet sat a pair of white skates with green laces and double runners. "But I need help getting them on."

"Lily, where did you get those?" Candace asked.

"They were over there with the other skates," Lily responded as she pointed to a spot about ten feet away. There sat two more pairs of skates, one with red laces and the other with gold. Candace and Parker skidded their way over to them, where Candace carefully bent down to pick up the smaller pair.

"What do you want to bet these fit me perfectly?" she asked to no one in particular.

"Like I said," Parker replied with a smile, "nothing should surprise us anymore." He grabbed the last pair as he carefully shuffled over to the ledge where Lily waited. Before trying on his own skates, he helped Lily into her right skate and began lacing it up tight. Candace arrived a moment later and did the same with Lily's left skate. Soon all three had donned their skates which, as Candace predicted, fit them like a glove.

"Have either of you skated before?" Parker asked. "Every winter I play broom hockey with my friends."

"I took figure skating classes for a couple of years when I was little," Candace said. "But it's been a while."

"I've never skated before in my life," Lily told them. "Is it hard? I don't want to fall."

In response, Candace and Parker each stood up and took one of Lily's hands in their own. They cautiously glided to the center of the chamber, pulling her between them. "Practice moving your feet while we pull you," Candace told her. "When you think you can do it on your own, let us know."

"Now that you're all set," Sprig told them, "the question is which direction we go."

"I don't think we have much of a choice," Parker said. "There's only one way out of this room. I'm guessing it won't always be that way though."

"Only one way to find out," Candace said. "Are you ready?"

Parker was instantly steady on the skates and Candace's body soon remembered its youthful lessons, so they easily began to glide out of the room into what resembled a long corridor of ice, with cold, tall walls rising close on either side of them. Lily tried her best to skate on her own but soon found it easier to hold on tight to her siblings' hands and let them do all the work.

The trio began to pick up confidence and speed, but as they veered around a bend to follow the path, a stalactite appeared immediately in front of Parker, causing him to yelp and quickly fall onto his back to safely slide under it.

"Maybe we should be in a little less of a hurry," he said

as he stood up and brushed ice off his pants. It turned out to be good advice. Stalactites and stalagmites began to appear almost out of nowhere on a regular basis. Sprig tried flying ahead to act as a scout, but her shouted warnings were lost among the echoes of the cave and she soon gave up.

Several minutes later the group emerged into a smaller chamber where the path they'd been following split into two like the upper part of the letter 'Y.' In the gap between the two routes sat a snowman about six feet tall with long twigs for arms, black charcoal eyes, a carrot nose, and six small, round pebbles arranged in a smile for a mouth. In the middle of its stomach where a person's belly button would be was a circular cavity with a red metallic surface.

"This is weird," Parker said.

"At least you didn't say 'whoops,'" Candace quipped.

"Which way do we go?" Sprig asked.

"Do we flip a coin? Make a guess? Take turns choosing?" Candace responded.

"Ask the snowman," Lily joked as she tentatively practiced moving forward on her own, two inches at a time.

Candace and Parker looked at each other, the same thought occurring to them simultaneously.

"Not a bad idea," Parker said. "I mean, it must be here for a reason. There's lots of ice here but no snow, and no pebbles, so it's not something a bunch of kids randomly built. And where it's placed, it does look like a traffic cop. The problem is, its arms point in two different directions."

"Agreed," Candace said. "And remember what the mage said? 'Trust the snowmen.' But assuming the answer to which direction we take is up to the snowman is one thing. Figuring out how to get it to reveal its secret is another."

"And the fact she said 'snowmen' plural means we're sure to encounter more than this one," Parker added. "So we need to get this right." The group assembled in front of the snowman and stared at it, looking for a clue. Sprig flew around the back but found nothing but more snow.

"He looks like just a regular snowman to me," Lily said.

"Not quite," Parker said. "And the answer might be hanging around Candace's neck."

Candace's hands flew instinctively to the amulet she'd forgotten she was wearing. She pulled the chain off and held it in front of her. "It does look like it'll fit," she said. "Here goes nothing." She moved closer to the snowman and inserted the amulet's ruby side into the red cavity in its stomach, then jumped back in anticipation.

For a moment, nothing happened. No explosion, no hidden chamber opening. The snowman didn't begin talking. But then its left arm began slowly moving across its chest to the right until it joined its other arm in pointing in that direction.

All four cheered as one. Candace gave a thumbs up gesture to Parker and they began gliding into the chamber on their left, the snowman's right. She and Parker occasionally let go of Lily to give her a chance to skate on her own but found it slowed them down. It was only a couple of minutes later that they came upon another chamber with a Y-shaped split and a snowman in the middle that was a twin of the first one.

Candace, impatient to leave the ice cave, wasted no time in using her amulet to initiate the snowman's signal. This time, its right arm moved to point to the snowman's left, the group's right. They headed that way.

Twice more the group came upon snowmen and twice more they followed the snowman's lead. They were growing restless, wondering how much longer this would go on. They reached a fifth snowman, which directed them to their left. Three of them began moving that way, but Candace remained behind.

"Parker, wait," she said. "Something's not right. 'Trust the snowmen' wasn't all the mage said to us, was it?"

Parker slowly skated back, dragging Lily with him. "No," he admitted. "She said trust 'all but one.' What are you thinking?"

"Something just feels different," she said. "That's all I can tell you."

For a long time, no one said anything, they just stared at the snowman. "We're fools," Candace finally said. "Everyone close your eyes and think back to each of the previous four snowmen's faces. Sear that image into your mind. Ready? Now open your eyes and look at this guy's face."

"What do you know," Parker said.

"It was so obvious," Sprig added.

"Its mouth is different," Lily said. "It has too many stones."

She was right. This snowman, unlike the others, had seven pebbles making up its smile instead of six. Sprig flew up to its face and pried the extra stone away, letting it fall to the icy floor. Candace reinserted the amulet in its stomach and the group watched as both of the snowman's arms moved to point the group to their right.

They quickly exited the chamber and two turns and one more snowman later, emerged through an opening onto a snowy field, the lights of something gleaming in the distance. Parker and Candace gave each other a high five, everyone switched out their skates for their boots, and the group started hiking in that direction.

Thirteen

Themselves

What from a distance appeared to be a village turned out to be only four small, identical cottages arranged equal distance apart to form a sort of circle, with all of them facing inward toward a square. In the middle of the square sat a miniature version of a train station with four small benches positioned exactly as the cottages were. The train tracks from the station led to a circular track running past the front doors of the cottages. To Lily's delight, a tiny train pulling four open coach cars slowly made its way around the tracks.

"'Welcome to Themselves,'" Candace said, reading a festive wooden sign that stood just outside the circle of homes. "What an odd name for a town, if that's what this is."

"They look like tiny playhouses," Lily said as they moved into the square. "They're not much taller than I am." The children gazed upon the cottages. One was green with red trim, a yellow door, and a blue roof. Moving clockwise, the next one was red with green trim, a blue door, and a yellow roof. Then a yellow one with blue trim, a green door, and a red roof. Finally, a blue one with yellow trim, a red door, and a green roof. The benches near the train station were all painted the same colors as the home they were aligned with.

"Who do you suppose lives here?" Parker asked. No sooner had he spoken than five little people emerged at the same time through their front doors, one each from three of the cottages and two from the last one. Like the benches, they were dressed to match the color scheme of their homes. Their pants, which blossomed out like bloomers, were the color of the home, their shirts that of the trim, their boots and mittens the same as the doors, and their stocking hats, cascading down their backs and ending in a white puff, were of course the colors of the roofs. The hats had slits on each side of the head, out of which poked the top of sets of pointy ears. "Elves," whispered Sprig.

Without seeming to recognize that they had company or acknowledging each other, the four stood perfectly still as the train made its way around the tracks, each one boarding a separate car. It took less than a minute to complete the circle, at which time they all got off and in a straight line stood in front of the group, who'd been too engrossed in the travel ceremony to say a word. Candace noticed they were lined up boy-girl-boy-girl-too hard to tell.

"You're late," said the elf on the left.

"Yes, yes, very late," said the next.

"But not too late," said the elf in the middle.

"No, just in time not to be too late," said the last two in unison. Their voices, which began sounding like that of a young child with the first elf, rose in pitch with each successive speaker until the pair on the end were a squeak that was painful to the ears.

"I'm Mize," said the first.

"Herz," said the second.

"Himz," said the third.

"Arz," said the pair.

"Both of you?" asked Candace. They nodded.

Parker took the lead and introduced he and his companions. "If you were expecting us," he said to the elves, "do you know why we're here?"

"Looking"

"For"

"The"

"Box," they said in sequence.

"Can you help us find it?" Lily asked.

Her question was met with silence, the elves glancing at each other uncomfortably and fidgeting. Then at some unheard signal, they gathered in a huddle, excited but indecipherable whispers reaching the ears of the children. Sprig tried to fly close to hear but was shushed away. After what seemed like ages but was closer to forty seconds, they broke the huddle. This time they stood in a single file line, one behind the other, as they faced the group. The first elf stepped forward.

"You may think our color scheme is strange," he said before stepping aside to give way to the second elf.

"But you best learn how we did arrange," she said, also moving to give the third elf room.

"For if a beast you soon meet delves," he said.

"You'll need a memory of each themselves," said one of the pair.

"Name time!" chirped the last elf.

The elves proceeded to call out their names, at first in order then at random. "Mize," "Herz," "Himz," "Arz." "Himz," "Mize," "Arz," "Herz." And on they went for exactly sixty seconds before falling silent, turning around in unison, and marching to the train that awaited them. Each deboarded in front of their own cottage and without looking back at the children, walked inside and closed the door.

"Wait!" called Parker. "We don't understand. Please explain what you just said."

"It's no use," Candace bemoaned. "They said what they needed to say. What do you think their poem means?"

"I think they said we'll meet a beast who's going to ask us something we need to remember," Sprig said. "Not a very cheerful prospect."

"I'm guessing we need to focus on the first two lines," Parker said. "If we assume it's telling us to do exactly what it says, we need to memorize how the elves arranged their colors. The pattern of their palate, I guess."

"Agreed," Candace responded. "I don't see how else we could interpret it. So what, we need to remember all of these color schemes? And which elf has what? That would take forever."

"Not if we all take one," Parker said. "That we should be able to do. Let's move to the benches and take the corresponding home. And remember the name of which elf you're doing too."

They did exactly that, sitting in silence only broken once when Candace commented that she tried to make it easier by remembering the colors by pairing them with a fruit, before realizing that apples and grapes come in almost every one of the colors. After a long period, Lily broke the silence.

"I can't sit any more. I'm going to remember. Can we go?"

The others looked around and nodded. "I don't think even a few more minutes is going to make any difference," Parker said.

They stood and began walking down the road that left the enclosure on the other side of where they'd come in, each one muttering colors under their breath.

Fourteen

Trolls and Bridges

"At least we haven't had to choose between two directions," Parker said, trying to improve the mood of the group. They'd been trudging over the barren landscape for what seemed like a long time, and while no one spoke of it, they all had the feeling that they were getting close to running out of time. Beyond that, they were getting bored of reciting their respective color schemes. Candace, for one, wondered if the elves had played a trick on them and if they'd need to remember the colors at all.

Moments later the group reached the crest of a hill and, far worse than being faced with a choice of paths, saw that up ahead in a hundred yards the road ended at the banks of a raging river. As they got closer they could see chunks of ice hurdling down with the flow of the water, crashing on rocks and splintering into dozens of pieces before being carried on.

The section of the river where the road ended wasn't very wide, but too wild and the water too cold to try to forge it. Farther on, it grew progressively wider.

"Now what?" Candace asked. "I don't suppose any of you thought to bring along an inflatable boat."

"Too rough for that anyway," Parker said even though he knew she wasn't being serious.

"I think I see a bridge!" Sprig cried from far above them. "Way over there next to that large rock formation. Let me fly over there to make sure it's safe to cross."

The three children were happy to rest while Sprig did her reconnaissance but knew they couldn't afford to wait too long, so they were relieved when she returned. "I have good news and bad news," she said.

Parker groaned. "Really? You're going to do that to us?"

Sprig ignored him. "The good news is that the bridge looks to be in perfect condition and we could be on the other side within only a few minutes. The bad news is, that isn't a boulder. It's a giant troll guarding the bridge."

"A giant friendly troll or a giant mean troll who will eat us up or throw us into the river?" Candace asked. Sprig simply shrugged her shoulders.

"It's not like we have much of a choice," Parker said with a sigh. "C'mon, troops, let's go say hello to the troll."

With a total lack of enthusiasm, the wary group headed in the direction of the bridge. As the troll came into view, their hearts sank. He at least looked the part of a mean creature. Ten feet tall, as wide as a car, and ugly. His overly large, rounded head was bald on top but unwashed gray and white hair sprouted on all sides and fell past his shoulders. His deep black eyes were as big as saucers, his nose flat and wide, and his mouth filled with crooked teeth. He wore a soiled tunic that might have been red at one time long ago, and carried a primitive but frightening wooden club in his huge left hand. He held up his right hand to stop the group as they approached.

"Halt!" he commanded in a deep voice that echoed in their ears. "Who wishes to cross my bridge?"

"We're on a mission for Santa," Candace said with a quiver. "Please, sir, let us pass."

The troll stepped aside to reveal the entrance to the bridge, which was blocked by a creature the likes of which the children had never seen or even imagined before. Its body at first appeared to be that of a chubby puppy, but as they looked closer they could see it was covered in furry scales, and jutting out from its paws were long, sharp claws. Its tail was long and thick and extended across the entire bridge. Strangest of all was its head, which was round, plump and dog-like as it sat on a short neck, but its sharp pointed ears and snout were that of a dragon, with puffs of smoke rising from its nostrils with every breath. Its eyes, one deep blue and the other bright green, eyed the children suspiciously as they stared back at it.

"What is that thing?" Candace asked.

"Part dog, part dragon. I don't know, maybe a dragadoodle?" Parker replied.

Despite being frozen in fright by the beast, the group couldn't help but snicker. "Dragadoodle it is," said Candace. "Let's hope this is the last one we ever see."

Taking their eyes off the creature, their focus moved to the side of the bridge. There, resting on a platform three feet off the ground, was a wooden model of a house. As they children got closer, they could see that it was an exact replica of the elven cottages from Themselves except for the total lack of color and the four rounded holes in the home's door, the outside of the home directly above the door, the shutters, and the roof. Hanging from the platform was a wire basket filled with colored marshmallows in red, green, blue, and yellow. A placard acting as a welcome mat for the home read "Mize."

At first the group said nothing, waiting for the troll to speak. When he didn't, they took it upon themselves to figure out what to do.

"It's a puzzle," Parker said at last. "I think we need to use the marshmallows to match the colors on Mize's house. We put the marshmallow that's the same color as his door into the hole in this door, then do the same for the openings in the roof, trim, and house. If we get it right, we get to cross the bridge. Who had Mize?"

"I did," Candace said. "I knew the colors by heart earlier

but I'm so nervous now I can't be sure." With shaking hands she took a green marshmallow and placed it into the space above the door, followed by a yellow one for the door, and a red one for the trim. As she moved to place the blue one in the roof she hesitated, then pulled the red one out, replaced it with the blue, and put the red one on the roof. She stood back, waiting for something to happen.

With a roar, the troll swung his club at the home, shattering it into pieces. The dragadoodle guarding the gate roared as it raised up on its hind legs, long trails of flame shooting from its beak. Frightened, the children ran from the scene as fast as they could, moving quickly farther down the river. As they ran, the troll threw handfuls of marshmallows after them, which fell like large hail.

"I'm sorry," Candace cried. "I couldn't think with that thing hovering over us."

"It's okay, we understand," Parker said, patting her shoulder. "And look. We get another chance."

In front of them was another bridge being guarded by another troll, which if anything was uglier than the first one. The river was wider here, so the bridge was longer. Without speaking, the troll stepped aside to reveal another dragadoodle guarding the entrance. And once more, there was a replica of an elf's cottage. This one said "Herz."

"That's mine," said Sprig. "I'll need help with the marshmallows." She hovered in front of the home, directing Parker which marshmallow to place where. Three times she had him switch them around before going back to her original placement. As Parker dropped the green marshmallow into the roof, another loud roar came from beside them. The group shrunk back and began running as fast as they could down the banks of the river as the troll demolished the poor cottage. Again, a storm of marshmallows peppered them as they ran.

This time they weren't surprised to come upon yet another bridge, longer still than the last one as it stretched across the angry river. This troll was shorter but even wider than the others, as if it had been stepped on and squashed. His appearance would be comical except for his expression, which was far more fierce-looking than the last two.

"Himz is mine," Parker told the others. He was sure he was right, but within minutes the four were fleeing again as the troll smashed the cottage and threw marshmallows to the sounds or a roaring, barking dragadoodle.

By the time they reached the last bridge, they were discouraged. Each time they were confident they had the colors right and each time they had been wrong. They looked upon the troll, who was barely taller than they were. It was the dragadoodle that was huge, towering as tall as any of the previous trolls.

Now it all came down to Lily to remember the correct color scheme for Arz's house. "I'm scared," she said.

"Lily, we know you can do this," Candace told her. "Just close your eyes and remember. You can beat this troll." Parker and Sprig gave her words of encouragement as well.

With determination and no hesitation, Lily strode up to the model cottage, pulled four marshmallows out of the bucket, and immediately placed them into the holes. Blue above the door, yellow shutters, red door, and green roof. Then she jumped back and put her hands over her ears.

Instead of a roar and a smash, she heard a canine whimper as the dragadoodle came over to them, laid flat, and panted. "I think she wants us to hop aboard," Candace said. The children climbed up onto its back and held on tight as it half ran and half flew over the bridge far above the frozen waters below, depositing them on the far side. Parker, Candace, and Sprig hugged Lily tightly, told her what a brave girl she had been, and marveled how she put the right colored marshmallows into the right slots with the troll towering over her.

"I told you I was good at remembering," Lily said with a smile.

Fifteen

The Christmas Market

The landscape on the far side of the bridge was hardly encouraging. With the river behind them, all the group could see were snowy hills in every other direction. "I don't know if we just got a step closer or if we're moving farther and farther away from where we need to be," Parker said. "Any guess which way we go?"

Candace bent down to take a closer look at the snow beneath their feet. "Look," she said. "There are faint footprints and other tracks that look like the runners on a sled. I think we should follow these."

The others agreed, and off they trekked. Lily took the lead since she stood closer to the ground and, with occasional help from Sprig, could see the tracks more easily than the others. The tracks led them up one hill and down another, around trees that appeared out of nowhere, and directly over a small boulder where, oddly, the sled's tracks split with each one going on opposite sides of the rock. They eventually encountered a moose sleeping directly in their path but were able to pick the trail back up on the other side after quietly sneaking past.

They were growing weary as they climbed a particularly steep and slippery hill, but when they reached the top, they were rewarded with a dazzling display of lights, music, and the sounds of happy throngs of people. Below them stood a vast Christmas market with close to a hundred small booths selling ornaments, wooden toys, knitted sweaters and socks, dollhouses, blankets, hot cider, sweets, and so much more. Strings of colored lights in the shape of stars were strung between the booths and groups of carolers competed to see who could sound more angelic.

As they neared, the aroma of freshly fried apple cider donuts filled the air and mingled with the smell of grilled meat. "I didn't realize how hungry I am until just now. I need something to eat," Parker said, the bag of pastries buried deep within his coat pocket long forgotten. The others quickly agreed.

Smiling men and women handed them pouches of tokens as they entered the market. "For food," one of them explained. "Come back if you need more."

Soon the children were wandering the aisles, plates heaped high with steaming sausages, potato pancakes, crispy bread smothered in melted cheese, roasted almonds, and strudel. They stopped by a booth for hot cider to wash down the food and were rewarded with ceramic mugs, each decorated with a different holiday scene. At each station, they were given tickets along with their food. "For a prize drawing," one vendor told them. "In the square in ten minutes."

The crowd got thicker as they walked further into the heart of the market until they had no choice but to go with the flow of traffic and head in the same direction as everyone else. Unsurprisingly, they ended up in a small square lined with food booths. A woman with platinum blonde hair braided in intricate designs and wearing a flowing burgundy gown with white puffy trim at the collar, wrists, and hem stood on a stepladder at one end of the square. She struggled to make herself heard, so the children maneuvered through the crowd to get closer.

"We have three prizes to raffle off today," she announced. "We have this basket courtesy of our wonderful food vendors." She held up a wicker basket almost as wide as she was tall, crammed with cheeses, fruit, nuts, candy, and an assortment of cookies. Transparent bags of cocoa mix lined the edge. "Then we have this basket courtesy of our delightful holiday shops." The children looked on transfixed as she displayed a basket gleaming with beautiful glass ornaments in all shapes and sizes, a warm winter scarf with matching hat, and an assortment of small toys and knickknacks. The crowd murmured excitedly at its sight. "Then finally, we have this anonymous donation," she said. She held up a poorly wrapped package that looked like it had barely survived the journey to the market. A tiny red bow ripped in several places was taped to its top. The crowd fell silent.

"The winners will get to choose in the order in which they're announced," the woman went on. "Please pull out your tickets." She held up a shiny black boot, reached in, and retrieved a slip of paper. "Our first winner is...number 818!" A disappointed crowd sighed in unison, looking around until they spotted an old man, hunched over with age and weighed down by the multiple layers of sweaters he wore, making his way to the front. To no one's surprise, he chose the basket of ornaments and toys.

"Our next lucky winner is number 7!" the woman called. A shriek of delight came from just to her left as a woman holding a child in each arm awkwardly held a ticket up into the air. She chose the food, telling everyone within hearing distance that she'd never won anything before.

The crowd began to disburse before the woman on the ladder could call the final number, leaving only a few dozen onlookers. Undeterred, the woman's hand dived one more time deep into the boot, where she swirled it around before grabbing onto a ticket. "And our final winner is...number 599!" she called.

"That's me!" Candace said to the delight of her companions. She walked up to the woman in charge, who by now had descended the ladder. "I won!" Candace told her, holding out her ticket.

"Yes, you did," came the reply. "And here's your prize.

Remember when you open it, that not everything is as it appears, and the reward is often the journey itself." With that the woman flashed the edge of her gown over her face and disappeared.

The children were mystified and looked around to see if the rest of the crowd had witnessed what they'd just seen, but to their surprise the square was empty. They began to walk back into the aisles of booths, but every one of them was shuttered and the entire market seemed deserted. "Listen," Sprig said.

Only then did they hear a very distant jingling. "It sounds like sleigh bells, or at least what I imagine them to sound like," Parker said.

The sounds grew progressively more distinct until they could make out movement down one of the aisles. As they watched, the moose they'd seen sleeping earlier emerged, a collar of brass bells hanging from its neck. More bells lined its harness, and red patterned leg wraps gave it a festive look. It was pulling a shiny red sleigh with gold runners that rose into elaborate curves, and was decorated with large green bows on its side. As it came even with the group, the moose stopped, looked in their direction, and snorted.

"Well, it beats walking," Candace said as she climbed aboard.

"No argument here," Parker said, lifting Lily up before he joined them. All three sat facing forward, squeezed close together, snuggling under a blanket that had lined the seat.

Sprig joined them, perched on the front of the sleigh. No sooner had they seated themselves than the moose took off at a slow pace.

"What did you win, Candace?" Lily asked.

"Oh! I'd almost forgotten with everything that happened," Candace replied. "Thanks for reminding me." She pulled the tattered package from the pocket of her coat, took off one mitten, and gently pulled the tapes off as the others looked on.

They all gasped. Sitting on her lap was a small wooden box about two inches high with a carving of a sprig of mistletoe on the top. For at least a minute, no one said a thing, staring at Santa's box in wonder.

"Open it up," Parker said. "Let's see what we've been chasing."

"Santa told us not to," Candace reminded him. "We have to wait." And so they rode over the river and through the woods to the sounds of jingling bells, hoping the moose knew which way to go.

Sixteen

The North Pole

As they traveled in the sleigh, the group could see that had they been left on their own to find their way back to the North Pole, they never would have found it. The moose picked up speed as it deftly navigated the sleigh over hills, around icy ponds, and through dense forests as the children huddled under the blanket to fend off the chill. They were grateful they were moving swiftly, as they had no concept of how late it was, so the real question was how much longer it would take to get to the North Pole.

Not too long, as it turned out. After dodging a small mountain of snow, the travelers found themselves speeding and skidding across a frozen lake. Lights in the distance were a welcome sign of civilization and as they got nearer, a sparkling star atop a tall Christmas tree peeking above the buildings forming a square looked familiar to Candace.

"We're here!" she cried. "Back at Santa's home!"

"Really?" Lily asked excitedly as she stood up to see better. "Do you think we'll meet him?" It dawned on Candace that she'd picked up Lily in the land of the fairies, so that she may never have been to the North Pole or met any of its inhabitants besides Sprig.

"I'm sure of it, assuming we got here on time," Candace answered. "He'll want to see that we retrieved his box."

The sleigh glided into the square and came to a stop at the base of the tree. Gone were all the wrapped gifts that had been piled high there earlier that day when Candace walked past on her way to Santa's workshop. As the children exited the sleigh, they looked around in confusion. They weren't sure where to go and, unlike that morning, there was no one around to ask.

"I'll see if I can find someone to bring you to Santa," Sprig told them before fluttering away. Soon afterward, a figure made its way toward the group. It was a woman adorned in a red dress visible beneath the open heavy coat that she looked to have thrown on quickly.

"There you are," she said kindly. "Santa's been so worried about you. I'm Mrs. Claus. Follow me. Quickly, now."

She led them to a nearby cottage, pushing open a heavy wooden door with a wreath of pine cones hanging on its front, and bid them inside. The room looked nothing like it had when Candace had been there earlier in the day. It was now furnished with comfy couches and a low wooden table between them. Across the room standing near a blazing fire in a fireplace as tall as he was paced Santa, paging through a thick book as he walked. His eyes gleamed when he saw who had entered the room.

"Just in time!" he roared happily. "In another hour you would have missed me."

"Why? Where are you going?" Lily asked. Candace and Parker looked at her in disbelief. "Oh," she said. "Right."

The group moved together to meet Santa by the fire, feeling warm for the first time in forever. Candace dug into her pocket and brought out the box, handing it to him. Santa broke into a wide smile as he placed a golden strip into the book to mark his page.

"Need to give those kids on the naughty list a few more minutes to redeem themselves before I take off," he said with a wink. "Please, sit down. Did you gather any other items during your adventure? If so, please put them on the table."

It took a few minutes for the children to empty their pockets. Out spilled the mugs from the street market, the cocoa from the spice shop, the flask of cream and milk from the tea shop, chocolate bars from the sweet shop, a cinnamon stick from the library, syrup from the cottage, and pastries from the bakery. Both Lily and Parker were surprised to pull out handfuls of colored marshmallows that had fallen into their pockets after being bombarded with them by the trolls.

"Excellent," Mrs. Santa said. She scraped the frosted

topping of the pastries into a sugar bowl then gathered everything up in her apron and carried it out of the room.

"We went to a lot of trouble to get the box back for you," Parker said. "Can we at least know what's in it?"

Santa glared at Parker for an uncomfortable couple of seconds before breaking into a grin and laughing loudly. "I'm teasing you, of course you can. It may be the most important item we have here at the North Pole: the secret ingredient in the recipe for hot chocolate that's been passed down for countless generations. It wouldn't taste the same without it." When he finished speaking, Santa leaned forward to hold the box out for all the children to see, then removed the lid.

"It's empty," Candace sighed with disappointment.

"No, Candace," Santa replied softly. "It's as full as it's ever been. One thing you'll learn is that some of the most important things in life aren't visible and can't be held in your hands. This box was empty when you arrived this morning and now it's overflowing with the special ingredient. All of you did that."

Candace and Parker glanced at each other, then at Lily, as the realization came to them, and nodded their heads in silence. "I don't get it," Lily said.

"I'll explain later," Candace told her. Just then Mrs. Claus returned with the children's mugs, steam pouring out of them that filled the room with the smell of chocolate. "Hold on," Candace said. "We need to wait for Sprig."

"Sprig?" Santa said, puzzled. "Who or what is Sprig?"

"The fairy from your tree!" Candace replied.

Santa shook his head slowly. "No one by that name here. No fairies at all, in fact. Now I hate to leave you but I need to get ready. Enjoy your drinks."

The children settled onto the couch, pushing themselves closer together and holding hands as they snuggled under a blanket and stared into the fire, trying to figure out what had just happened. As they watched the dancing flames they sipped their hot chocolate, with the same thought running through each of their minds: that it was by far the best hot chocolate they had ever had. It was the last thought they had before waking up in their own beds on Christmas morning.

Back at the North Pole, Santa sighed in contentment as he entered his workshop. Looking up at the fairy ornament at the top of the tree, he nodded slightly and winked before placing the box carefully back at its place on the shelf, where it would remain safe for another year.

Six

Christmas

"The end," Dad pronounced.

For a while, no one said a word until Parker broke the silence. "Good story, Dad."

"Agreed," Candace added.

"I liked it," Lily said.

"Glad to hear it," Dad said as he rose to a stand. "Now you've waited long enough. How about some hot chocolate?"

"Don't you need to add the special ingredient?" Candace asked.

Dad smiled down at his children snuggled close together in front of the fire, contented expressions on their faces, sharing the same blankets and comforter. "Already added," he said, "while I was telling the story."

He went to the kitchen to grab some clean mugs, digging deep into a cabinet to find those he'd used as a child, each one of the four decorated with a different holiday scene. As he returned to the living room and began ladling steaming hot chocolate into the mugs, the lights in the house came on. "Ah," he said. "Kids, our Wi-Fi is probably back up as well if you want to get your phones."

In response, Candace rose, moved over to the light switch, and turned it off, plunging the home back into darkness except for the flickering of candlelight and the flames in the fireplace. She returned to her place in front of the fire next to her siblings and accepted a mug of hot chocolate from her dad.

With their first sips, their faces lit up. Parker stared into his mug, astonished. Lily just murmured her approval as she licked her lips. Candace continued to take small sips, looking puzzled before going back for more. Finally, she had to ask. "Dad, how—"

Before she could continue, Dad simply put his finger to his lips, and the children fell into silence, listening to the crackling of the fire. As they stared at the dancing flames, sipping their hot chocolate, listening to the wind outside hurl snow against the windows, the same thought ran through the minds of all of them. This was the best Christmas they had ever had.

Acknowledgment

I'm honored to have enlisted the limitless talents of my friend and collaborator Stephanie Rocha, who's tapped deep into her imagination to creatively capture the essence of this story in an exemplary explosion of image and color. With this little holiday fantasy, given free rein to express herself, she's managed to bring my words to life and in many ways outshine them with her whimsical illustrations. This wouldn't be the same book without her incredible contributions both in art and beyond. She has my deepest admiration and gratitude.

www.ingramcontent.com/pod-product-compliance
Lightning Source LLC
Chambersburg PA
CBHW052042280426
43661CB00084B/37